She
Who
Dwells

Overcoming
Fear and
Finding Peace

Jessica Landmon

Women Get Real
womengetreal.org

*To my incredible family who stood
by me through my battle with fear.*

*I am so thankful for my amazing children,
Brett and Jenna, who gave me a reason to
fight each and every day.*

*I also want to thank my parents who raised
me to be a strong woman of faith.*

*I especially want to thank my husband, Chad, for his
unconditional love and support. Thank you for your
patience, for leading our family well, and for standing
arm and arm with me in prayer.*

*Lastly, this book would not be possible without my
sweet Goldendoodle, Dakota, who literally sat on my
lap for most of the writing process, making writing
this book that much more difficult!*

Contents

Introduction

My twenties were awesome. Marriage, baby, then another baby, a new house, even a dog. Things were picture perfect. Then my thirties came creeping along, and everything I knew was challenged.

After an intimate season of prayer and fasting, I felt nudged to give God more of me. There were parts of me that I knew were not fully surrendered, and I wanted to be "all in." At that time, I was struggling with some small-scale fear issues—your typical mom stuff. But I later discovered that Psalm 91 was going to be the Scripture and work that God made real in my life as I learned how to fully trust Him and claim the promises found in this passage.

Now, God takes you seriously when you make declarations like the one I did. Consider yourself fairly warned. One month later, I found myself smack in the middle of my worst nightmare. I was in a crowded Las Vegas hotel attending my closest childhood friend's wedding, frantically asking strangers, "Have you seen my three-year-old daughter? She is wearing pink and she doesn't have any shoes on."

I was so careful, always watching my kids like a hawk, but my daughter's transition from me to my husband this time obviously did not go as smoothly as I had planned. I was numb, and I cried out to Jesus like never before. And He, as usual, was faithful. Five long minutes later, we were reunited. It felt like FOREVER. Now, a normal person would have responded with, "Praise God. Even when I fail, my God is gracious, and His blood covering prevails against any attack of the enemy." Well, I learned that I am anything but normal.

My fear multiplied. Instead of small scale "mom fear," a full spirit of "what if" entered my life. For those of you who don't know "what if," let me introduce you. He disrupts your peace and coyly whispers in your ears:

> What if something happens to my kids?
>
> What if I receive a bad diagnosis from the doctor?
>
> What if I can't pay my bills?
>
> What if another terrorist attack hits our country?
>
> What if my husband leaves me?
>
> What if I am alone the rest of my life?
>
> What if I fail?
>
> What if ___? You fill in the blank.

"What if" robs you of your sleep and your peace, a gift God so graciously gives to us. My journey with combating this demonic lie was a long journey because God loved me so much that He wanted to honor my heartfelt cry for full surrender and squeeze every ounce of fear right out of me.

The next few years I like to affectionately label the breaking years, where I spent most of my time fighting the lies of the enemy through constant prayer and recitation of Scripture. I had awesome times with the Lord, studying

His Word. But it was based on pure desperation, focusing on my weakness instead of the freedom that Jesus Christ had already given me.

It wasn't until I made a conscious decision to trust God at His Word that I became free. Psalm 91 felt like a love letter written directly to me from my Heavenly Father. I took hold of this passage of Scripture—read it, memorized it, and meditated on it day and night—until it became a reality for me. The words became alive, and His promises illuminated right before me on the pages of Scripture. The beauty here is that, although Psalm 91 is an Old Testament promise, we as New Testament Christians can still claim these promises. And with that, no matter what this life on earth brings us, we have eternal hope in the salvation that comes from Jesus Christ.

I pray that the truth of His Word will have the same transforming power for you as it did for me. As we take this journey together, we will learn practical techniques in how to get into the presence of God, what dwelling with the Father actually looks like, and how to trust the Lord at His Word. We are going to take a deep dive into the character, nature, and very heart of our loving Creator. Instead of being consumed by the "what ifs" of this world, I pray that you walk away confident and run into your Father's arms as you navigate the different seasons of your life.

You were never meant to live a life in bondage to the enemy, trapped in his lies and deception. Embrace the freedom that the Lord wants to give you so that you can live the life that God intends.

Psalm 91

¹ Whoever dwells in the shelter of the
Most High will rest in the shadow of
the Almighty.
² I will say of the LORD, "He is
my refuge and my fortress,
my God, in whom I trust."

³ Surely he will save you
from the fowler's snare and
from the deadly pestilence.
⁴ He will cover you with
his feathers, and under
his wings you will
find refuge; his
faithfulness
will be your
shield and
rampart.

⁵ You will not fear the terror of night,
nor the arrow that flies by day,
⁶ nor the pestilence that stalks in the darkness,
nor the plague that destroys at midday.
⁷ A thousand may fall at your side,
ten thousand at your right hand,
but it will not come near you.
⁸ You will only observe with your eyes
and see the punishment of the wicked.

⁹ If you say, "The LORD is my refuge,"
and you make the Most High your dwelling,
¹⁰ no harm will overtake you,
no disaster will come near your tent.
¹¹ For he will command his angels concerning you
to guard you in all your ways;
¹² they will lift you up in their hands,
so that you will not strike your foot against a stone.
¹³ You will tread on the lion and the cobra;
you will trample the great lion and the serpent.

¹⁴ "Because he loves me," says the LORD, "I will rescue him;
I will protect him, for he acknowledges my name.
¹⁵ He will call on me, and I will answer him;
I will be with him in trouble,
I will deliver him and honor him.
¹⁶ With long life I will satisfy him
and show him my salvation."

She Dwells

Whoever dwells in the shelter of the Most High

-Psalm 91:1

She Who Dwells is a woman who is steadfastly sure of God's undeniable love, unfailing promises, and divine plans for her life. There is no place for doubt or fear as she is cohabitating with the Lord Most High. The enemy knocks at her door, trying to entice her to fear and worry, but she doesn't answer. She has another appointment and has no time for unexpected drop-in guests. She escapes the cares and worries of the world and leaves them behind as she sits at Heavenly places with her Father. She has learned the secret of dwelling with Him.

That sounds like a dream! But what exactly does it mean to dwell? According to *Merriam-Webster*, to dwell means "to remain for a time" or "to live as a resident."[1] The image of a woman who dwells is beautiful as we put this in the context of the Scripture. We often crave the rest that is spoken of in the second part of this Scripture—"will rest in the shadow of the Almighty"—neglecting to focus that His provision is contingent upon our action. She who dwells in the shelter of the Most High will rest. Yes! But she must learn to dwell.

This concept of dwelling with God gets a little confusing for some as we literally aren't packing our suitcases and moving into God's house. However, we need to understand that our spirit should be. Our tendency must be to run to God and stay a while in His presence.

One thing I ask from the LORD, this only do I seek:
that I may dwell in the house of the LORD all the days
of my life, to gaze on the beauty of the LORD and to
seek him in his temple.
–Psalm 27:4

Don't let my last name Landmon fool you. I come from a super close-knit Italian family. We spend a lot of time together, to say the least. We enjoy being together, talking about our lives, laughing together, telling stories, and sharing our dreams. One of the ongoing jokes in our family comes from my mother. We could be visiting with her for hours on end, and without fail, she jests, "Leaving already? You just got here." Although we all laugh about it, these words have a powerful message.

Time goes by quickly when you enjoy the company you are with. Have you ever been with a friend thinking you had loads of time only to have to wrap it up quickly because time got the best of you? It amazes me how fast the clock ticks by when you are spending it with someone you want to talk to. There is always a longing for it not to end, for it to continue on.

God feels the same way about us. Many of us toss up a quick prayer in the morning, not to check in with Him until right before bed unless, of course, some major setback occurs during our day. God desires more time with us. I know there have been many incidences in my hurried morning prayers where I can almost hear God echo the words my mom says to us. "Leaving already? You just got here." Oh, how it must break His heart. He longs to spend time with us. Obviously, we cannot spend all day on our knees in quiet communion with the Lord, but we can live in a routine that is constantly in His presence.

Time in God's presence offers us an opportunity to connect with the Lord Most High. We get to—that's right, get to—sit with Him in Heavenly places. So often, we act like spending time with God is a chore or an item to check off our list before we can move on to the rest of our day. Rather, this is an amazing invitation to hear and listen to the heartbeat of God. In His presence, our focus changes as we align with His will and His plans. True time in His presence should be a continual act of worship, surrender, and listening, as we try to keep in step with Him.

> We get to—that's right, get to—sit with Him in Heavenly places.

And God raised us up with Christ and seated us with
him in the heavenly realms in Christ Jesus.
–Ephesians 2:6

I remember when I started dating my husband back in high school. Yes, we are high school sweethearts (insert aww now). I remember just longing to squeeze in any time together.

We would see each other in school, spend our afternoons together, and then when we got home, he would call me on the phone so that we could talk some more. We just loved spending every available moment together. We never got bored. We never ran out of things to talk about. We continued to learn new things about each other. We planned our future together and shared our hopes and dreams. It was a precious time. Still, to this day, my husband and I value our communication. It has been instrumental in keeping our relationship strong. We still plan together. We still dream together. And we love spending time in one another's presence.

God wants this type of relationship with you. He wants to dream with you. He wants to spend time planning your future, directing your steps, giving you guidance and wisdom as you navigate through your life. He is enamored with you and wants you to want to dwell with Him.

Knowing all this, why would we let anything get in the way of time with our Heavenly Father? Well, as a mom, wife, daughter, sister, friend, church member, pastor, and speaker, I recognize that life gets busy. I know all too well the demands that are placed on us. Everyone and everything seem to be screaming for our attention. Sometimes it is just easier to give oil to the proverbial squeaky wheel rather than prioritize what really matters. But we need to be intentional.

Intentionality seems to be the buzzword these days. We need to be intentional with our self-care, intentional with the foods we eat, intentional with setting goals and following through. And this is all true. But let us not forget that we need to be intentional about spending time with God. If we are not intentional, then it simply will not happen. If we don't set aside time each day to really bask in His presence, worship at His feet, and listen to His heart, then it will result in a quick five-minute mundane ritual that we check off our list each day. If we are not intentional about making time with Him a priority, then we will never learn the secret and the benefits of dwelling with Him.

You Must Come in Close to Hear God's Heart

Here is a little acronym that I came up with that will help you be more successful in your time with God. Without a plan, it is easy to get distracted and discouraged.

D .... *Direct*
W .... *Worship*
E .... *Expect*
L .... *Listen*
L .... *Linger*

The first thing you need to do is **direct** your thoughts toward Him. Release all your cares and worries to the Lord. Lay anything that occupies your mind space at the feet of Jesus. Is there a conflict with a coworker that is eating away at you? Are you concerned about your child's walk with God? Or are you simply overwhelmed with all the things that are piling up on your plate for the day or even the weeks to come? Whatever is burdening your heart in this moment needs to be released into Jesus's capable hands so that you can fully focus on your time with Him. For me, sometimes the best way for me to literally let go of the worries I am carrying is to write them down. It may seem like an unnecessary step, but there is something powerful about writing your concerns and worries on paper as a symbolic act of release.

> *Cast all your anxiety on him*
> *because he cares for you.*
> – 1 Peter 5:7

Now you are ready to **worship**. Worship isn't just the part of the church service where we sing songs, although if music helps you give honor and reverence to the Lord Most High, then by all means play it loudly. The time of worship is about recognizing and glorifying all that He is—His matchless love, His great gift of salvation, the gift of the Holy Spirit to walk with us and comfort us all the days of our lives. This time is all about Him and not about us at all. This is when we take our eyes off the situations in our lives and lift our heads towards Heaven in praise and adoration. I promise you that you will never run out of things to worship Him for.

> *"Yours, Lᴏʀᴅ, is the greatness and the power*
> *and the glory and the majesty and the splendor,*
> *for everything in heaven and earth is yours.*
> *Yours, Lᴏʀᴅ, is the kingdom;*
> *you are exalted as head over all."*
> – 1 Chronicles 29:11

The next step for a successful time in His presence is to **expect** God to show up. We serve a God who is alive and powerful. During our time in His presence, we should expect Him to move. We should expect Him to speak. We should expect Him to impart. The traditional Western way of prayer is to recite some written words that someone else composed and then move on with our day. This is not what God intended for us. He wants a conversation, not a request list. He wants to give you your fresh "manna" for the day. It is easy for us to forget that. We must expect more during our prayer time.

> *"'Call to me and I will answer you and tell you great*
> *and unsearchable things you do not know.'"*
> – Jeremiah 33:3

Once we have established our expectation level, now it's time to **listen**. Listen to all that God has to say. Listen to what He wants to impart to you. It's time for you to stop talking and allow Him to have His turn. Have you ever been around a person where you feel like you can't get a word in edgewise? Well, this is your opportunity not to be that person. For me, having a pen and journal handy is a great way to record all the secrets that He is sharing with me. I love to reference it later and see the progression of what God is doing in my life.

And remember, God speaks to us in a variety of ways. He speaks to us through dreams, visions, an inner knowing, and even an audible voice. But if you are having a tough time discerning if it is Him or you, then I encourage you to always start in the Bible, His Holy Scriptures. This is the timeless, infallible Word of God. Allow these words to penetrate your heart, refresh your soul, and transform your mind into the likeness of Christ.

> *For the word of God is alive and active. Sharper than any double-edged sword, it penetrates even to dividing soul and spirit, joints and marrow; it judges the thoughts and attitudes of the heart.*
> –Hebrews 4:12

Lastly, but certainly not least, it's time to **linger**. This is the part most people try to skip. Don't rush off. Try to enjoy the beauty of His presence. Be still. Bask in His love. Fix your gaze on Him. Experience His joy. Connect with His heart. In a world full of pressure to do and act and say the right things, just be for a moment. Enjoy the solitude of His presence. And don't let go. Hold on to it all day long, checking back in with Him as your day goes on.

> *"Be still, and know that I am God."*
> –Psalm 46:10

Remember, dwelling in God's house is not just a once or twice a week habit. Nor does it need to be a big production where you block off hours every morning. This must become a routine part of our lives if you want to live the life that God intends. And before you get completely overwhelmed, I am not suggesting that you spend two hours every morning before work in prayer and supplication (although that certainly can be beneficial). It is quality not quantity. But we will never experience the supernatural peace that He alone offers if we do not understand and practice this discipline. Remember, we don't have to; we get to spend time with our Heavenly Father.

Mary Chose What Is Better

As Jesus and his disciples were on their way, he came to a village where a woman named Martha opened her home to him. She had a sister called Mary, who sat at the Lord's feet listening to what he said. But Martha was distracted by all the preparations that had to be made. She came to him and asked, "Lord, don't you care that my sister has left me to do the work by myself? Tell her to help me!"

"Martha, Martha," the Lord answered, "you are worried and upset about many things, but few things are needed—or indeed only one. Mary has chosen what is better, and it will not be taken away from her."

–Luke 10:38-42

This is a principle that Martha learned progressively through the pages of Scripture. As women, we can often get caught up with the doing part. I think there is a little something in each of us that makes us feel important or worthy when we can put a big checkmark next to something on our to-do lists. In fact, I sometimes struggle with the bad rap Martha gets for feeling miffed that her sister wasn't helping out. Someone had to feed all those guests! And from what I gather from Scripture, those disciples could eat. As someone who entertains often, I know what planning and preparation goes into successfully pulling something like this off. The meal wasn't going to just supernaturally appear (although Jesus was in the house).

> *I think there is a little something in each of us that makes us feel important or worthy when we can put a big checkmark next to something on our to-do lists.*

Now, would I have gone to Jesus and tattled on Mary? I sure hope not, but I do understand Martha's frustration. In full transparency, I tend to be more of a Martha. I am a doer, albeit doing things for God, but a doer. There are times when I am racing against the clock, trying to fit in all that needs to be accomplished. I would love to just sit at Jesus's feet and listen to His teachings and His stories.

But like Martha, I often feel the pressure to perform rather than to dwell because people are expecting me to. Did you get that? I feel the pressure of other people's expectations.

But here is what I have learned—if you want to tackle the to-do list, you must sit with Jesus first. It's arrogant of you to think that you can actually accomplish anything without first sitting at the feet of Jesus and spending time with Him. When you make that a priority, He will go with you and help you accomplish all that you need to do. And the beauty is that when you invite Him into your day, He will make you more efficient and less stressed and give you the wisdom to let go of things you were never meant to do. It's not that you don't have the time to sit with Jesus; it's more like you don't have the time not to. Ladies, we must learn to dwell with Him. ✤

GOING DEEPER

1. As you read the opening paragraph, meditate on the characteristics of a woman who dwells and reflect on your own life. What are some of the things in your life that are keeping you from dwelling in the presence of God (time, fear, lack of know-how, entertainment, etc.)?

2. Martha, like many of us, felt the intense pressure to produce. In a world full of Martha-like expectations, how do you carve out time to experience Mary-like moments before you tackle your day? What strategies have been successful? Which ones have not?

3. We know that it is in the stillness that God strengthens His people. Why do you think it is so hard to linger in God's presence and wait on Him?

4. When was the last time you had an intimate time of prayer with the Lord? How did your day unfold as a result of putting Him first?

She Rests

Will rest in the shadow of the Almighty

–Psalm 91:1

Did you know that people spend approximately sixty-five billion dollars a year on sleep products[1] to ensure a good night's rest? High-end mattresses, deluxe mattress pads, expensive pillows, high thread count sheets, sleep masks, tranquil music, meditation apps on your phone—the list goes on and on. Why is there such an upward swing in these purchases? It's simple. Our rest is being compromised. We are running at one hundred miles per hour, trying to juggle balls that we were never meant to juggle, all in an effort to finish a race we weren't meant to run in the first place.

But I have some fantastic news. All the investments in products may help, but you will never get the rest you were meant to get until you learn to dwell in the shelter of the Most High. God's house will always provide us with the best night's sleep. His sheet thread count is probably over two thousand, His pillows are perfect, the mattress firmness is spot on, and the room temperature is always just the way you like it. In all seriousness, all our cares and worries will simply fade away as we learn to rest in the lap of Yahweh, basking in His security.

"Come to me, all you who are weary and burdened,
and I will give you rest."
–Matthew 11:28

A sign hangs above my dresser in my bedroom that reads, "Give It to God and Go to Sleep." It is the last thing my eyes see before I close them at night. This sign reminds me that before I try to sleep, before I make any attempt to get a good night's rest by my own efforts, I need to unburden my heart before the Lord. I need to spend time in His presence and release all the worries and strains from that day into His hands.

As a mom, I have lived this out first hand. I remember instances when my kids were upset or concerned about something that would tug at their hearts. It wasn't until they were able to release it to me that they felt relief. In my hands, they knew that everything would be ok. I recall one incident in particular where my daughter was involved in a she said/she said situation. Oh, the drama with girls! Fortunately, my daughter was not directly involved, but two of her friends were. I vividly remember all the emotions and tears that were involved with this young teen encounter. My daughter unloaded it all on me, every last detail. I listened intently to all her concerns, and then I assured her that even though her attempts to fix it had failed, it was now time for me to get involved. Once she heard those reassuring words, the burden was lifted from her instantaneously, and she was able to rest knowing that I had it under control. This was no longer an area that she needed to concern herself with.

You see, my daughter has faith in me. She knows that I will do the right thing because she knows how much I love her. She knows that I only want good for her and not harm. She knows my character because she spent loads of time with me. She had watched me intercede before, and she was confident I would take care of it again. My daughter slept great that night as she rested securely knowing that this was now my battle, not hers. The same is true with our Heavenly Father.

> *The trials we walk through when released into God's hands no longer are our battle to fight; they are now His.*

As we unload all the cares of the world into His capable hands and spend time being built up in His presence, we can sleep like He intended us to. We can achieve a perfect rest. The trials we walk through when released into God's hands no longer are our battle to fight; they are now His. But we must release them.

Cast all your anxiety on him because he cares for you.
– 1 Peter 5:7

Rest Is No Joke

Rest tends to be a joke these days with competing catch phrases like "You only live once" or "I will sleep when I'm dead." The world would tell you to chase every opportunity placed before you, work yourself until you are sick, because if you work hard, you can play hard. But rest is important to God. He created mortal beings with a capacity for only so much. Proper rest is an integral part of our mental and physical health. Carrying the burdens and stresses of the world will slowly lead us down a road of self-destruction. And the worst part of all of this is that God wants to take all these burdens from us so that we can enjoy a peace-filled, anxiety-free life.

Right at the very beginning in Genesis, Scripture recaps the account of creation. Reflecting back to my Sunday school days, I remember being taught that God created the world in seven days. However, that's incorrect. He created the world in six days, and on the seventh day, He rested. Yes, God, the supreme ruler over all, rested. He ceased to work. He stopped and reflected on what He had done. Did God need to rest? I highly doubt that. However, He wanted to model behavior that we would copy.

"The Sabbath was made for man,
not man for the Sabbath."
– Mark 2:27

In the New Testament, Jesus communicates to His disciples the importance of a sabbath day and clearly depicts it as it is—a gift from God to His people to release them from the burdens of life. We need to be careful not to become legalistic about it, but rest is something that our Heavenly Father wants to gift us. And not just one day a week, but every day, as we spend time dwelling with Him. He wants us to feel safe. He wants us to feel seen and heard and held in His arms. We have to stop looking to the world for rest for our souls. Do you wonder why you never feel at peace, why you constantly feel overwhelmed or weighed down? God is the only thing that will give us what our spirits so deeply crave.

I love this illustration that new mom and podcaster Tori Masters writes about her son, Micah. The comparison of a baby intimately knowing his mother is exactly the kind of relationship God so desires to have with us. But this kind of relationship can only be achieved by spending time with Him.

My baby RESTS in my arms because he knows me...my heartbeat is familiar to him...even in the dark, he knows my voice and studies my face with his tiny little hands...he knows that in my embrace he will be covered, protected, fed, nourished, comforted, and taken care of. When he is hungry, tired, scared, uncomfortable, or unsure, he looks to me, and when I am not around, he looks for me. When he sees me his eyes light up because he knows he is loved by me. He mimics my expressions and is impacted by the mood.

*My baby knows that he doesn't have to offer me any-
thing or "produce" anything in exchange for my love
and devotion to him...This feeling, this security, this
love that my baby has come to know is how we should
feel as CHILDREN OF GOD.[2]*

His Shadow

I don't just want to focus on the rest portion of this
Scripture. I'd like to discuss the shadow piece, as well.
The imagery the psalmist uses is simply beautiful. Have
you ever thought about how big God's shadow actually
is? I can't even begin to imagine. We have a pool in our
backyard that we spend a good portion of our summer
enjoying. For years, we did not have any areas of shade
around it, except for some canopy that the trees provided
in the late afternoon as the sun moved behind them. It
wasn't much, but it did create some form of relief. This is
good news for keeping your pool nice and warm in New
England, but bad news for those who need a reprieve
from the scorching, hot rays.

When my kids were little, I was always right in the pool
with them, splashing about, playing games, and staying
wet and cool. But as they got older, the pool was overtaken by a bunch of teenagers, and now, my job was to
sit on the sidelines and provide a watchful eye and nothing else. Let me tell you, the absence of shade became
unbearable on those hot summer days. The necessity
of an umbrella became quickly apparent. In an extreme
knee-jerk reaction, I ordered a thirteen-foot umbrella. I

know that sounds a little obnoxious, but it provides an amazing escape from the blazing sun. And let me tell you, it made all the difference for me, as there was now a ten-degree cooler atmosphere under that thing. I could stay outside all day long under its protection.

Now, ladies, if a simple umbrella can do all that, can you imagine the shadow that the Most High can cast? My mind is blown away just thinking about what the psalmist is trying to convey in the first verse of Psalm 91. I know this all sounds figurative, but these are promises from God to help us find the peace and security that the world simply cannot offer us. But we have to learn the secret of dwelling with Him. The sheer implication of Psalm 91:1 is that this life will have troubles! We need to learn the principle of dwelling with Him so that we can find rest for our souls, our minds, and our bodies blanketed underneath His vast shadow.

God does not want you to be stressed! Read that again. God does not want you to be stressed! He wants you to trust Him. As I said earlier, the burdens most of us carry have physical and mental consequences. "More than three-quarters of adults report symptoms of stress, including headache, tiredness, or sleeping problems."[3] These are just some of the minor side effects of carrying stress inducers. Stress can also contribute to more serious conditions like heart disease, depression, and even cancer. Stress-induced sickness and poor emotional well-being are more prevalent now than ever before. But God has a solution, and it is rest. But we have to go to His house to get it.

For in the day of trouble he will keep me safe in his dwelling; he will hide me in the shelter of his sacred tent and set me high upon a rock.
−Psalm 27:5

A little exercise I like to do when I am feeling stressed, overwhelmed, or anxious about anything is to grab a piece of paper and make a list of all the things that are burdening my spirit. This practice alone can often lift some of the worry off of your shoulders, but I encourage you to take it a step further and ask the Lord what He has to say about all those things that are crowding your heart and mind.

For example, if you are worried about your finances, then scour your Bible or search the internet for all Scriptures regarding money and finances.

"Bring the whole tithe into the storehouse, that there may be food in my house. Test me in this," says the LORD Almighty, "and see if I will not throw open the floodgates of heaven and pour out so much blessing that there will not be room enough to store it."
−Malachi 3:10

"For where your treasure is, there your heart will be also."
−Luke 12:34

And my God will supply every need of yours according to his riches in glory in Christ Jesus.
−Philippians 4:19 (ESV)

Here are just a few of the many Scriptures pertaining to money and finances. Learn them. Write them down. Meditate on them. Determine if there is an area of your life where you are not honoring God with your money. Are you tithing? Is your heart putting too much value on wealth accumulation? Are you putting your trust in material things rather than the things of God? Allow the Word of God to expose areas where your heart isn't right, then correct them. If there is no correction needed on your part, then start declaring these promises over your life. These Scriptures aren't "fortune cookie" promises that may or may not come true. They are promises given by God Himself for His people. Receive them in faith.

Finances are not the only things that keep us up at night. Here are Scriptures for some of the common areas that can cause stress in your life:

Anxiety

Do not be anxious about anything, but in every situation, by prayer and petition, with thanksgiving, present your requests to God. And the peace of God, which transcends all understanding, will guard your hearts and your minds in Christ Jesus.

–Philippians 4:6-7

Sickness

But he was pierced for our transgressions, he was crushed for our iniquities; the punishment that brought us peace was on him, and by his wounds we are healed.

–Isaiah 53:5

Loneliness

Draw near to God and He will draw near to you.
–James 4:8 (ESV)

Even though I walk through the darkest valley, I will fear no evil, for you are with me; your rod and your staff, they comfort me.
–Psalm 23:4

Weariness

Let us not become weary in doing good, for at the proper time we will reap a harvest if we do not give up.
–Galatians 6:9

Confusion

"But when he, the Spirit of truth, comes, he will guide you into all the truth. He will not speak on his own; he will speak only what he hears, and he will tell you what is yet to come."
–John 16:13

Insignificance

"Look at the birds of the air; they do not sow or reap or store away in barns, and yet your heavenly Father feeds them. Are you not much more valuable than they? Can any one of you by worrying add a single hour to your life?"
–Matthew 6:26-27

Temptation

*No temptation has overtaken you except what is
common to mankind. And God is faithful; he will not
let you be tempted beyond what you can bear.
But when you are tempted, he will also provide
a way out so that you can endure it.*

– 1 Corinthians 10:13

Persecution

*But you, LORD, are a shield around me, my glory,
the One who lifts my head high.*

– Psalm 3:3

The Bible, the Holy Scriptures, is our handbook for life. All of the answers to any of our problems are found there. We must learn what the Word of God says about our situation and believe that those promises are true for us. Stop running to self-help guides, other religions, food, alcohol, drugs, unhealthy relationships, and any other temporary fixes. Instead, set your face towards the Father, unburden your heart (just like my kids have done to me), and release your cares into His capable, loving hands. Experience His presence, feel protected by His massive shadow, and know that you are loved. Now, rest well, sweet friend. ෴

GOING DEEPER

1. What strategies have you previously tried to ensure a restful night's sleep? Were these strategies effective? Why or why not? Do you think that ending your day spending time with your Heavenly Father will help you sleep better?

2. Why is knowing the character of God so important to our faith?

3. In what areas do you believe your health is being compromised as a result of failing to rest?

4. Does knowing that God does not want you to be stressed change how you will try to manage stressful situations in the future? What ways have you been successful? What strategies do you still need to implement?

5. What specific areas in your life right now are causing you the most stress? Find three Scriptures from the Bible that teach you what God has to say about that matter.

She Trusts

I will say of the LORD, "He is
my refuge and my fortress,
my God, in whom I trust."
–Psalm 91:2

Refuge and fortress are terms that sound straight out of medieval times. However, in Biblical terms, they should, once again, be a resounding assurance of a God who provides peace and safety to the ones He loves. God wants you to remove yourself from the chaos and the storms of the world so that you can clearly hear the gentle voice of a loving father bending down low to whisper in your ear, "I got this. You are mine."

Let's dissect this a little further, starting with the word "refuge." Refuge is "a condition of being safe or sheltered from pursuit, danger, or trouble."[1] My friends, there is a real enemy out there whose very job description is to "steal, kill, and destroy you" (John 10:10). Let there be no mistake: The devil hates you and is trying to deceive you, harass you, ruin your life, and rob your peace! That sounds harsh, but it is the absolute truth. Once you begin to understand this, you will see how important this promise from God is.

Isn't it absolutely amazing to think that we can find refuge from these attacks in our Heavenly Father? In the midst of the worst of days, we have confidence that we are safe and sheltered. We need not fear the enemy's pursuit because God has put a shelter around us, a literal hedge of protection.

Finding Your Refuge

The hurricane season of 2022 started off with a bang. Hurricane Ian literally ripped apart Southwest Florida, leaving a path of destruction in its wake. Warnings kept going out to find refuge in a safe place as a Category 4, almost 5, hurricane approached the coastline. In fact, the National Weather Service issued this general advisory for storm protection: "Take refuge in a small interior room, closet, or hallway on the lowest level during the storm. Put as many walls between you and the outside as you can."[2]

When the storms come, we need to find a place where the wind, rain, and storm surge can't harm us. Especially to those living along the coast or in low lying elevations, heading to a place of refuge could mean the difference between life and death. The same is true for a Christian.

When the storms of life come, and they will, we need to take refuge. We often default to trying to protect ourselves or fix the situation in our own strength, but we need to do just the opposite. We need to lock ourselves in a small room—some might call it a prayer closet—creating a spiritual barrier between us and the storm that is brewing all around. When we commune with the Lord, something happens in the supernatural realm—a shield of protection envelops us, keeping all danger at bay.

This is a perfect illustration of God's desired relationship with us. He wants us to release the difficulties into His hands as we rest in His love, bask in the truth of His promises, and meditate on the security of His faithfulness. He is trustworthy. If there is one thing that you pull away from this chapter, it is just that—God is trustworthy. I know people have failed you. I know that you have been let down, but our God is trustworthy! When doubt tries to settle in, remember God has never failed you. The great theologian, preacher, and writer A. W. Tozer says this: "While it looks like things are out of control, behind the scenes there is a God who has not surrendered His authority."[3] God has full authority over you and your circumstance. Trust Him!

> *If there is one thing that you pull away from this chapter, it is just that—God is trustworthy.*

Finding Your Fortress

Refuge and fortress seem to be basically the same thing, but there is a small difference. Refuge is the person or place you run to, while fortress is a fortified dwelling often used in military terms. When I say the word fortress, what comes to your mind?

When I surveyed a group of women, this was their initial response:

- Protection
- Solitude
- Safe place
- Unbreakable shelter around me
- Secure dwelling

All of these are spot on. But there was one woman's response that made me take pause. When asked what do you think of when I say the word fortress, she replied, "A fortress is the hedge of protection, that wall of fire that is set around me."

Can you just picture that for a moment? I know we live in a very three-dimensional world, but we can't ignore the fact that there is a spiritual world happening all around us that we cannot see. There is a battle every day in the heavenlies over our protection. To recognize that there is a literal hedge, a wall of fire, surrounding me each day that the enemy cannot penetrate puts my heart at ease. There is a secret place surrounded by His glory where I get to dwell, and the enemy can't touch me. Hallelujah!

So how do we get to this secret place, you might ask? We must create it.

Let's talk about Susanna Wesley, mother to the great theologians John and Charles Wesley. These godly men focused heavily "upon the role of the Holy Spirit in the life of the believer."[4] Charles is also credited with writing over 6,500 hymns, some of which we still sing today. In addition to these two sons, Susanna birthed seventeen more children, some sadly dying during infancy. Needless to say, her house was a busy one. Susanna took care of her children's needs and provided an excellent education to all her children, including her daughters. And if that wasn't enough, she supplemented their spiritual teachings because she felt that there was not enough diversification in the teaching taught at church. Susanna initially intended to just offer deeper instruction for her family; however, once the word got out about what she was doing, nearly two hundred people attended her teachings each week. To say she was a busy woman is an understatement. How could she juggle all this? Susanna understood the importance of finding her secret place, her refuge and fortress from the world. If she was going to pour out, she must first be poured into. She needed time in God's presence.

Susanna didn't have a special room designated solely for prayer. She didn't even have a prayer closet with a door. She lived in a one-room home. What Susanna Wesley had, however, was a makeshift fortress that she could escape to each day and meet with her Heavenly Father. Susanna was a woman who learned how to find that secret place and dwell with Him.

Mother Wesley's solution to this was to bring her Bible to her favorite chair and throw her long apron up over her head, forming a sort of tent. This became something akin to the "tent of meeting," the tabernacle in the days of Moses in the Old Testament. Every person in the household, from the smallest toddler to the oldest domestic helpers, knew well to respect this signal. When Susanna was under the apron, she was with God and was not to be disturbed except in the case of the direst emergency. There in the privacy of her little tent, she interceded for her husband and children and plumbed the deep mysteries of God in the Scriptures. This holy discipline equipped her with a thorough and profound knowledge of the Bible....

Susanna passed away in 1742 at the age of seventy-three, living long enough to see her sons John and Charles become world-renowned leaders of the global Christian movement. This is her legacy, forged in large part in those diligent hours of intercession under that makeshift apron tent.[5]

When I learned how Susanna fought to have time in God's presence, I felt so guilty and convicted. It makes all my excuses fall to the wayside when in my comfortable, daily life, I sometimes can't find time to spend alone with Jesus. Susanna had every reason and excuse to rationalize skipping her quiet time, but she knew in her heart that this discipline would be life giving. Susanna wouldn't allow anything to prioritize itself over her time in the fortress. Those prayers uttered in her makeshift tent had significance far beyond what she could ever imagine. Those prayers were foundational to a massive Christian movement. Those simple prayers had eternal value all because she faithfully spent time in her secret place with her Heavenly Father.

Where is your secret place? Maybe it's a chair in your bedroom where you love to read the Bible. Perhaps it's in your closet, away from the messes and distractions of your home. Or maybe you are like Susanna Wesley and you find a chair in the middle of the room and throw an apron over your head to commune with the Lord Most High. The truth is, it really doesn't matter where your secret place is, as long as you have one. And when you find it and learn how to regularly have time in His presence, your life and the life of your family will be transformed.

In His presence, all fear is gone. When fear is removed, trust exponentially grows. The unknown no longer becomes worrisome because you know that God is on your side, and He has "'plans to prosper you and not to harm you, plans to give you hope and a future.'" (Jeremiah 29:11).

"But blessed is the one who trusts in the LORD, whose confidence is in him. They will be like a tree planted by the water that sends out its roots by the stream. It does not fear when heat comes; its leaves are always green. It has no worries in a year of drought and never fails to bear fruit."

–Jeremiah 17:7-8

Do You Trust Me?

I don't know about the rest of you, but one of my favorite Disney movie moments is when Aladdin extends his hand to Jasmine and asks, "Do you trust me?" I get goosebumps just thinking about it. In fact, this moment happens twice in the movie. The first time, the palace guards are chasing the two of them on the rooftop, and there appears to be no way out. Aladdin offers her an unseen method of escape. The second time occurs when Aladdin offers to take Jasmine out of the palace and on an extraordinary adventure by way of a magic carpet. In both situations, the only thing preventing her from escaping is her—that is, her ability to put her faith in him. Jasmine needs to trust Aladdin completely.

This iconic movie moment has obviously made a lasting impression on me. You see, when I am going through a trial in my life, or when I am simply feeling overwhelmed, I sometimes feel like I am being closed in on all sides, and there is no natural way out. It is in those moments when I hear the Lord whisper in my ear, "Do you trust me?" It is now up to me as to what happens next.

It is crazy to think how much we limit God's ability. We often look for solutions in the natural, and when there isn't one, we assume there is no solution. How small-minded we are! God created the Heavens and the earth, breathed life into man, parted the Red Sea, raised people back from the dead, healed all sorts of sick people, and even moved the sun backward ten steps, just to name a few. After hearing all that, do you honestly think that there is something in your life that is out of the realm of God's ability? Do you really think God is up in Heaven scratching His head, thinking, "She got me this time. I simply don't know how to fix this." That's ridiculous to even say out loud!

God loves you with an extravagant love. And He only wants what is best for you. You need to trust Him.

Several years ago, when my kids were still in the toddler stage, I found a suspicious lump on my right breast. After a quick examination from my doctor, she sent me for further testing. She was feeling confident that it was nothing to worry about, but not confident enough to rule out anything serious without a mammogram and ultrasound. Anyone who has walked through these types of moments knows how much anxiety there is while waiting to schedule the tests and receive the results.

What did I do? I dug into the Word of God and tried to reject any negative thought that came my way. And yet, I still felt like a constant burden was pressing down around me as I awaited the results. The devil would come and whisper all sorts of worst-case scenarios into my ears, trying to rob me of that day's joy. Interestingly though, it was during this season of life that the Lord brought me to Psalm 91 and taught me about the secret place—a place where I can dwell and feel no fear because His presence overpowers me. The secret place has been my go-to escape in times of trouble or turmoil. The beautiful thing is that my Heavenly Father is never too busy to meet me. He is always there waiting like a good Father with open arms ready to wrap around me and tell me everything is going to be ok. And it was.

But here is the lesson we must take away from this because this is the lesson the Lord wanted me to learn.

He wanted me to trust Him for a good report. And, He wanted me to be so secure in His love for me, that I could trust Him even if I got a bad report. He wanted me to know that no matter what happened, He was in it.

My test results were actually very delayed, and I truly believe that it was because He wanted to stretch my faith a little further. As I waited and spent time with God, I felt no fear because I believed that my results would come back benign. Interestingly though, that wasn't enough for God. He wanted me to trust Him no matter what. He wanted me to trust Him for a good report. And, He wanted me to be so secure in His love for me, that I could trust Him even if I got a bad report. He wanted me to know that no matter what happened, He was in it.

Five years after this testing and now in my mid-thirties, I needed to go back for my baseline testing. This time, I wasn't nervous at all. I had really learned the secret of dwelling with Him and felt no fear. Now, the way my imaging center works is that they send you a letter in the mail with your results after the radiologist reviews your images. It could take a few days to process. To be honest, I went for the test and had completely forgotten all about receiving the results. I clearly had come a long way.

As I drove up to my mailbox a few days after the test, I heard the Lord ask me those iconic movie words, "Jessica, do you trust me?" Not thinking at all about the test results, I immediately responded back with an emphatic yes! "Jessica, will you still trust me if they found something?" This yes was a little weaker but still genuine.

I opened up my mailbox, and you guessed it, the results letter from the imaging center had arrived. Sure enough, they found a suspicious area on my mammogram that needed further testing. Instead of getting rattled like the old Jessica would, I remembered Psalm 91:2—"'He is my refuge and my fortress, my God, in whom I trust'"—and peace flooded my heart. Instead of defaulting to panic mode, I ran to my secret place and felt His loving presence surround me.

Once again, my God was faithful and kept me from a fiery storm. Some may wonder why I even had to walk through this again? What was the point of it? God was interested in the condition of my heart. Was I only at peace because everything was going fine in my life, or was I at peace because I knew my Heavenly Father was in charge? I often warn women that after you pass a test, God often gives you a surprise pop quiz to make sure you are walking in the same powerful truth that He first brought you to.

So, ladies, do you trust Him? I mean do you really trust God with your life? Do you trust Him to deliver you from the storm, and do you trust Him to walk you through it? Do you trust Him with your future? Do you trust Him with your health? Do you trust Him with your finances? Do you trust Him in your marriage? Do you trust Him with your children? If there is any hesitation to these questions, ask yourself why. Where are you putting your trust? Who are you making your refuge and your fortress? Listen, we can do all the right things, eat all the right foods, do all the right exercises, and see all the fancy doctors, but your future is ultimately in His hands. Do you trust Him with it? ✍

GOING DEEPER

1. Do you believe that God is trustworthy? Why or why not?

2. Where do you spend your quiet time with the Lord? Does it encourage you to learn that Susanna Wesley was able to find a space where she could commune with God alone even though she lived in a one-room home full of kids and distractions?

3. Susanna Wesley left a remarkable legacy. What kind of legacy do you want to leave when your time on this earth is done? What changes in your life must you make today to ensure a lasting impact?

4. Do you believe that there is anything outside of God's ability to fix? Why do we need to walk through trials and storms in the first place? Think back to all the times where God has moved in your life. Write them down and thank Him for His faithfulness.

5. Why do you think God wants us to trust Him "even if"? What does that say about our faith?

She Is Safe

Surely he will save you from the fowler's snare and from the deadly pestilence.

-Psalm 91:3

Surely is a word that is used to express complete confidence and assurance that what is said will certainly happen. When someone uses this word, there is no doubt, absolutely none, that what they are saying will come to pass. It gives my heart great pleasure knowing that when I read the word surely in Scripture, what comes next is reliable and true. The writer of Psalm 91 clearly had confidence in his safety as he prefaces this promise with surely.

Now, let's talk about that fowler. That's a fun word we don't use too often these days. For those of you who don't know, a fowler is simply a person who hunts fowl or birds. The fowler uses all sorts of tactics to bait the birds into his trap or net. Each type of bird, however, may require a different technique in order to catch them.

Did you know that a chicken can run faster than the average human? It amazes me to think that those tiny little legs can out run mine, but it is true. So then, how does a fowler catch a chicken, or any other fowl for that matter? Strategy!

If you research fowler techniques, which I doubt you have, you will soon discover that there are several effective strategies for catching fowl, which vary based on the type of fowl you are targeting. What works to catch a tom turkey is different than what works to catch a gander goose. I bet you feel enlightened already. There apparently are three main tips for capturing a bird.

First, you must consider the flight zone, which is "the area surrounding an animal in which a person can approach before the animal moves away." If you get too close too quickly, the bird will retreat, and you'll have lost your opportunity. Instead, "move slowly and steadily, and avoid abrupt or sudden motions."

Second, "the easiest, most efficient way to catch birds is to corral them into a corner and reduce the amount of space to escape." When you force a bird into a space that has no exit, your chances for grabbing one is high. The bird feels hopeless, and just retreats. In some instances, an emboldened bird may fly at the fowler offensively, escaping the almost inevitable clutches of his hand or net.

And finally, the last technique for catching a bird focuses on the time of day for trapping, which has a great impact on the success of a catch. The best time to attempt to catch a fowl is at the end of the day. When the bird is "more docile...instinct drives them to seek a safe nesting place or area to perch for the evening. Therefore, birds are easier to catch once it is dark." The bird is lulled into a false sense of security when it retreats to its nest, making it easy prey for the fowler.[1]

We obviously are aware that the psalmist isn't promising safety from an actual fowler, but rather the fowler is a symbol of a predator looking to catch its prey. The predator, in this instance, is the devil, and you, my friend, are the prey. The devil is on the prowl to destroy you. We have already established that. This Scripture promises us that God, our faithful Father, will save us from Satan's snare. Satan's devices are crafty and timely, but not at all original. He continues to reuse and recycle his same old tricks over and over again. We have assurance that our Father will keep us safe in His care.

> *Be sober-minded; be watchful. Your adversary the*
> *devil prowls around like a roaring lion, seeking*
> *someone to devour.*
> – 1 Peter 5:8 (ESV)

The interesting thing is that the tactics the fowler uses to capture the fowl are not much different than the tactics that the enemy uses to trap us. Did you notice the similarities as you were reading them? Let's quickly go through them so that you are wise to the fowler's—or in our case, the devil's—schemes.

Flight Zone

The devil is well aware of your flight zone. If he comes too close too quickly, you will be wise to his schemes and know to run away. However, in his crafty and cunning ways, he knows to slowly and methodically edge his way closer and closer to you until you are helpless and fall victim. The devil will never try to tempt you straight out with big sins; instead, he convinces you that small compromises in your faith really aren't that bad.

Once the "smaller" sin grasps ahold of you and becomes commonplace, he then tempts you with bigger and bigger compromises until you are so far away from your faith that it becomes too hard to return. Then, he knows that he's got you. If we do not keep our spiritual guard up, we will fail. The Christian walk has no room for compromise.

Let's talk hypothetically about Krista. She loves movies and entertainment. It's her retreat—her place to escape the cares and worries of the world. Her schedule has been so busy the last few months with work and chauffeuring her kids around that her Bible time and devotional time has lessened. She is exhausted. Can you blame her? It's much easier to plop on the couch at the end of a busy day and just watch television rather than spend time in the Word.

As you are well aware, television shows today are increasingly filled with sex and crude language. Krista is a Christian and knows that this behavior and language are completely unacceptable, but the shows she watches are entertaining. And, after all, she's not the one sinning.

Krista rationalizes watching the shows because she needs a release. She thinks it is harmless. A small compromise in this area may not seem like a big deal to most, but not surprisingly, over time, Krista's behavior is being affected. Some of the language Krista has heard from her shows is now commonplace in her vocabulary. She is now watching movies that are not only "grey," but are blatantly inappropriate. All of sudden, Krista finds herself struggling with lust and is tempted in this area.

You see, the enemy would have never tempted her with pornography and foul language straight out of the gate. He knew she was too smart for that. He tempted her slowly but methodically until her guard was down, and she didn't even realize that she was being preyed upon.

Once the frog fell in a vessel of the hot water. The Water was still on a gas stove. The frog still did not try to jump out of the vessel, instead just stayed in it. As the temperature of the water started to rise, the frog managed to adjust its body temperature accordingly. As the water started to reach the boiling point, the frog was no longer able to keep up and manage its body temperature according to the water temperature.

The frog tried to jump out of the vessel but with water temperature reaching its boiling point, the frog was not able to bear it and couldn't make it. What was the reason that a frog couldn't make it? Will you blame the hot water for it?[2]

This child's fable really drives my point home. The frog should have jumped out the minute he fell into the pot. But the water felt nice, and he thought he had plenty of time to jump out later. We cannot allow ourselves to tolerate any part of sin, and when we are given the opportunity to walk away, we must. Scripture promises that God will always provide a way out, but we need to take it. He will save us from the fowler's snare, but we need to be obedient and listen to His warning signs when it is time to leave.

> *God is faithful; he will not let you be tempted beyond*
> *what you can bear. But when you are tempted, he will*
> *also provide a way out so that you can endure it.*
> – 1 Corinthians 10:13

Cornering Method

The enemy also utilizes the cornering method, just like the fowler does. He intentionally boxes you into situations that seem impossible to escape. We spend too much time fighting the devil defensively, forgetting that we have an offensive game to play as well. The only effective strategy in this instance is to rebuke the enemy in the name of Jesus and regain our position of authority.

I liken it to a boxing match. I grew up watching the Rocky movies. Inevitably, in every movie, Rocky Balboa, a.k.a. the Italian Stallion, gets pinned in the corner against the ropes as his opponent barrages him with a series of powerful blows. It appears that Rocky's opponent has the upper hand, but as signaled by the change of music, Rocky is invigorated and begins to transition into an offensive game. With powerful force and determination, Rocky changes the trajectory of the boxing match and, in most cases, wins, or at least "goes the distance." Just because the enemy has you cornered doesn't mean that he will be victorious. We still have one more trick up our sleeve.

Just because the enemy has you cornered doesn't mean that he will be victorious. We still have one more trick up our sleeve.

The enemy would love to box you in a corner and steal your hope, making you think that there is no way out of your impossible situation. One of the saddest things that happens to Christians today is they forget the power and authority that they actually carry. Jesus handed that authority over to us so that we can be victorious in this world. Unfortunately, we have forgotten to use this power and authority effectively.

> *"I have given you authority to trample on snakes and scorpions and to overcome all the power of the enemy; nothing will harm you."*
> —Luke 10:19

Knowing that we carry this power and authority, we need to exercise it. Spirits of depression, anxiety, and fear must bow to the name of Jesus. You have authority over them. It means you have the power to lay hands on sick people, and they will get well. It means that you can speak into your hopeless marriage or financial hardships, and they will be miraculous restored.

Time of Day

The last strategy I want to discuss is probably one that most of us will fall victim to. The fowler doesn't attempt to trap the birds when they are attentive and full of energy. He waits to the end of the day when the birds are tired, worn out, and inattentive. This is when we need to be the most mindful of the schemes of the enemy. He knows when we are the weakest, and that is when he will pounce, trying to trap us.

I recognize that the end of my day is definitely when I am the most vulnerable. I am tired and worn out. The idea of putting my pajamas on, throwing my hair up in a messy bun, and just letting my guard down after a long day sounds so appealing. But this is when we need to keep our spiritual guard up the most. It's the time of day when we need to stay plugged into the source. It's time to reconnect with the Lord so that we are not victims to the enemy's ploys. It's in these hours of the day when quarrels begin, hurtful words are spoken, sound judgment is down, and poor decisions are made. In this part of the day, we need a whole lot of Jesus.

Satan is always a fowler. Whatever his tactics may be, his object is still the same—to catch men in his net. Men are here compared to silly, weak birds, that have not skill enough to avoid the snare, and have not strength enough to escape from it. Satan is the fowler; he has been so and is so still; and if he does not now attack us as the roaring lion, roaring against us in persecution, he attacks us as the adder, creeping silently along the path, endeavoring to bite our heel with his poisoned fangs, and weaken the power of grace and ruin the life of godliness within us.[3]
— *Charles Spurgeon*

His Power Knows No Boundaries

We've dodged that crazy fowler, but what about the deadly pestilence? As is the case from the fowler, the psalmist emphatically promises that God will surely save you from the deadly pestilence. Pestilence is "a contagious or infectious epidemic disease that is virulent and devastating."[4] Unfortunately, I think we all are a little too familiar with pestilence these days. Psalm 91:3, however, assures us that we are safe. God will protect us and save us from all of these things. However, what we cannot conclude is that we will not face them. If we didn't face these trials, why would we need saving in the first place?

God is sovereign. We need to have faith in Him and trust His plan above our own. We need not worry about the days ahead because we have surrendered them into the Lord's hand, but that doesn't mean it's going to be all puppies and rainbows. I wasted so many years worrying about all the diseases and sickness that I could get. The enemy used every symptom I encountered as a weapon to torment me and cause me to think that something bad was going to happen to me. All that did was cause stress and robbed me of my peace.

Interestingly, it was when I was really set free from the enemy's mind games that I got the dreaded call from the doctor that I used to fear. After a few months of dealing with severe and unusual inflammation, my doctor and my blood tests concluded that I had rheumatoid arthritis. Even though autoimmune diseases are not technically an infectious disease like a pestilence, they are becoming increasingly common these days. In fact, one out of every ten people now have some form of autoimmune disease, which can be debilitating or lead to premature death. And although there are a lot of prescriptions on the market to treat the symptoms, it is very difficult to get the right balance of medicines, and there is no known cure. In the case of rheumatoid arthritis, the disease attacks and destroys all the small joints in the body and possibly some organs. This certainly isn't a prognosis you want to receive.

I'm not going to lie. This was a really difficult season for me. My symptoms intensified quite rapidly. I'd wake up each morning unable to open my hands because the inflammation was so bad. Every joint in my body constantly ached, making the simplest of tasks difficult—getting dressed, walking down the stairs, brushing my teeth, making dinner, and even typing on a keyboard. I quickly learned how to do life in constant pain, smiling because

I really didn't want anyone to worry. My doctor wanted to immediately put me on high doses of medicine, but the side effects seemed worse than the disease. Although I am not against medication in any way, these immune suppressants only promised relief for a short period of time until the next level of drugs would be needed.

This was all transpiring so fast. One day, I went to bed healthy; the next day, I woke up sick. None of this made any sense. I felt like I had aged thirty years in just a couple of months. I was too busy with work for the Lord to have to deal with sickness. This was not part of my plan.

I remember one particular day in the midst of all this uncertainty, standing inside my doctor's office in excruciating pain, listening to him describe the severity of my condition. I could see his mouth moving, yet I truly was having trouble processing all that he was saying. It felt like a bad dream. All I could do was retreat to my Heavenly Father. I was looking at my doctor, nodding my head, but under my breath, I started declaring the promises of Psalm 91 that got me through other difficult seasons of my life. As I prayed, my faith began to strengthen. I remembered who I was and, more importantly, whose I was.

I remembered who I was and, more importantly, whose I was.

This disease didn't take God by surprise. He hadn't relinquished control over my life. God was still in charge. And right there in my doctor's office, I heard God audibly speak to me with the most loving voice, "Jessica, remember I have the last word. Don't receive this." That's all it took—a moment with my Heavenly Father changed the whole direction of my life. "Surely, He would save me from the deadly pestilence" (Psalm 91:3). He promised. And He did just that.

I will spare you the long and drawn out details, but basically, I am a walking anomaly. I prefer to say that I'm a walking miracle. My blood tests still show that I have the disease. My rheumatoid factor numbers are still extremely high. But my doctor is baffled as to why I no longer have any symptoms, especially because I had such a severe case. God did an amazing, supernatural work in my body. Did it take some cooperation on my part? It always does. I have completely changed my diet and agreed to take some low dose medicine, but I am symptom free because of Jesus's healing hand. Hallelujah!

I hung on to this promise with everything I had, believing that the Lord would do what He said He would do. He is our Savior. He is our Rescuer. And the same God that saved me can save you from whatever you are walking through. We can focus on all the impossibilities of the situation, or we can recognize that the Creator of the universe has another move He can make. The best part is that He doesn't need to play by the rules of the universe that limit us. His power knows no boundaries. Our Heavenly Father always has the last word. He will save us! ✍

GOING DEEPER

1. When you look at the tactics the devil uses to trap us, what methods have you recognized that he has tried on you? Where are you the most vulnerable?

2. After reading the story about Krista, are there areas in your life you can now identify as areas of compromise? If so, what are you going to do to stop the enemy from moving in on you?

3. Luke 10:19 clearly states that we have been given authority to defeat the enemy. As you examine your life and the current battle you are going through, are you walking in your God-given authority? If not, how can you start to exercise this authority in your everyday life?

4. What time of day are you at your weakest? What habits are you going to instill to prevent yourself from the attacks of the enemy?

5. A moment with my Heavenly Father changed the whole direction of my life. This statement is not just true for me, but for everyone. Are there any health issues you are facing right now where you need God to show up? Have you surrendered them to Him?

She Is Shielded

He will cover you with his feathers, and under his wings you will find refuge; his faithfulness will be your shield and rampart.

-Psalm 91:4

Some of my fondest memories growing up are those playing with my older brother. My brother wasn't one of those mean, bossy, older brothers that are sometimes depicted on television shows, but rather a true lifetime friend that God gifted me. To this day, there isn't a day that goes by that I don't talk to him. In fact, he and his family literally live two minutes away from me.

When we were younger, we would play all sorts of things together. His friends were my friends. My friends were his. I wasn't against catching a football in the backyard, and he wasn't afraid to extend his pinky at a proper tea party. However, like with all siblings, we sometimes would annoy one another. Unfortunately, this usually occurred in a long car ride or while shopping for furniture.

I can remember certain instances where we would literally get on each other's last nerve. Most of it occurred out of pure boredom. Why stepping on his foot made the situation less boring, I'm not really sure now, but it seemed so at the time. In those moments, poking, bumping into each other, tickling, and who knows what else was all fair game to make the time go by quickly. But in hindsight, the strangest things would happen if it got out of hand and one of us didn't want to engage any longer. We would simply declare: "Shield!" And for some reason, that was enough to stop the other person from continuing down his/her annoying path.

Ridiculous, right? Why would a simple word stop all the shenanigans? There was no physical shield that miraculously developed. Nor was there any real consequence to violating the shield rulebook. However, that was the rule of the game, and we both knew it and obeyed it.

And so it goes with the devil. He will try his hardest to launch every single attack your way. He is not full of mercy or compassion, thinking, "Well, she's had enough." His job description is "'to steal and kill and destroy'" (John 10:10). He is relentless, and to think otherwise is foolish. However, just like my brother and I, the devil knows the rules of the game, and he MUST play by them. When we exercise authority and rebuke him in the name of Jesus, the devil must flee. He must! It's not his game, but he must play by God's rules.

As we discussed in the previous chapter, too many Christians are walking around completely unaware of the authority they carry. Jesus clearly has given us His authority, and yet we don't truly understand what power we carry. I don't know about you, but I don't want to give the devil any more territory. He's taken enough. I'm tired of seeing people robbed of God's blessings because we aren't exercising the authority and power that Jesus gifted us.

I touched on the incident that sparked fear in my life in the introduction. Now, I'd like to talk to you about it from the perspective of my daughter. But first, let me explain something. Each and every day, I pray a covering—a shield—around my children. I pray that the enemy would have no position in their life. I declare the Scripture that no harm will touch them as they are surrounded by God's love and protection. I don't ever underestimate the enemy's tactics, and I certainly recognize the protection that our powerful God provides.

When all this transpired with my daughter in Las Vegas, my heart was in panic mode. It was racing. It was like a bad dream. Everything seemed to slow down, yet

> When we exercise authority and rebuke him in the name of Jesus, the devil must flee. He must! It's not his game, but he must play by God's rules.

everyone around me seemed to be moving at normal speed. All I could do was literally speak the name of Jesus. I was so overcome with emotion that I didn't have the strength or the time in that moment to do any sort of spiritual warfare. I just kept saying over and over again, "Jesus, please help!"

I frantically ran down the corridor of the Venetian hotel in Las Vegas, hoping to catch a glimpse of my baby girl. Now, if you are at all familiar with this hotel, or any property in Las Vegas, you know the enormity of these hotels. They are gigantic. The Venetian is filled with shops and eateries all along a makeshift canal of running water. My mind was full of concern that maybe she fell in the canal, or worse yet, she was grabbed by someone and would never be seen again. This happened almost seventeen years ago, and yet my heart goes right back to that moment when I think about it.

Interestingly, as my husband and I were screaming her name in panic, she was having a delightful stroll through the hotel. No fear. No worry. Not a concern in the world. After a tip that someone had seen her up ahead, I ran as fast as I could to get her. And then, I saw her. I burst into tears, screaming, "Thank you, Jesus," for all to hear. I quickly grabbed her, sobbing uncontrollably at this point, expecting her to be terrified that she made this long journey alone. Well, I couldn't have been more wrong. She seemed surprised that I was upset. She looked at me without an ounce of fear and said, "I couldn't find Daddy." "I know," I wanted to retort back. But instead, I asked her if she was scared or afraid or hurt. What she said next blew me away. "Mommy, why would I be afraid? Jesus was with me the whole time."

"You mean, you felt Jesus?" I quickly asked. "No, He walked with me," she replied.

All those prayers each and every day to protect my kids from harm were not done in vain. When I failed, He did not. He was faithful. I couldn't be there, but He was. Later that day, I ran into the couple who gave me the tip as to where she was. They obviously were overjoyed that we found her. They told me how weird it was to see this little girl push through the busy Venetian hotel untouched. And they said, and I quote, "It was like there was a shield or bubble around her. No one could get near her."

When we fail, He is faithful. When we aren't enough, He is!

His faithfulness will be our shield and rampart.
– Psalm 91:4

Let's Talk About Those Feathers

This part of the Scripture projects such a beautiful image of a momma bird shielding her baby under her wings— the perfect depiction of parental love. I have heard it said that the composition of a bird's wing is actually like a weather dome, shielding the baby from the elements. The baby bird is completely sheltered and cared for.

Are you not feeling another bird/fowl illustration? Me neither. Let's try the romantic movie route instead. A rainstorm appears out of nowhere. Clearly, neither have a weather app on their phone because they are caught completely by surprise in a torrential downpour without an umbrella. The gentleman opens his coat, pulls the woman in close, and shields her from the rain. It is a beautiful moment of love and protection.

We need to understand that as the mother bird shields her baby under her wing for protection, it also creates a stronger bond between the mother and the child. The baby bird is so close to the heart that she hears her mother's heartbeat. Put another way, the one shielded feels every breath and hears the heartbeat of her protector. In stormy seasons, we shouldn't just run for protection, but run for intimacy too. We should be so close to God that we can know His heart and feel it beat.

I have a toy goldendoodle. She is just the sweetest thing. All eleven pounds of her wants to be near me all the time. In fact, I've written most of this book with her draped across my lap. She has taken lap dog to a whole new level. She shows affection in the most adorable ways. If I am sitting on the couch, she quickly jumps up right next to me, drops her head, and nuzzles up as close as she possibly can, as if we were attached. I like to think that's what God wants from us. To purposefully get as close as we can to Him, as if we were one.

Psalm 91:4 offers so much more than protection from danger. It is an invitation to connect with our Father in a beautiful way. Imagine laying your head on His shoulder, His arm circling around you. All your worry and stress simply melt away. You are held. Things that were once unclear, confusing, or didn't make sense, all become clear as you connect with Him. This is the perfect love that John talks about in the New Testament. This type of love is why our fear should disappear.

> *There is no fear in love. But perfect love drives out fear, because fear has to do with punishment. The one who fears is not made perfect in love.*
> – 1 John 4:18

I think that sometimes we as Christians get so lost in reading and memorizing Scripture that we forget the very character of our Heavenly Father who wrote them. We can often feel unseen and ruled, rather than loved and cared for. God loves us individually. It may be hard for some to understand this type of unconditional love if the relationship with your earthly father is broken. But God's love is not conditional. It is not moody or contingent. It is eternal, and it is yours for the taking.

There Is a Lion in the Camp

I recently returned from a humanitarian trip to Malawi with an organization called charity: water. This organization brings fresh drinking water to impoverished villages throughout Africa, Southeast Asia, and South America. The experience, as you can imagine, was truly life-changing. Toward the end of the trip, when the site visits were complete, our team drove to Malawi's Liwonde National Park for a two-night safari. The camp where we stayed was small and intimate, consisting of only ten chalets scattered along the Shire River right in the center of the reserve. Our team occupied the entire camp. Because of our proximity to the wildlife, we were explicitly warned not to go outside without an escort after dark, just in case an animal was hiding in the darkness. If we needed to leave for any circumstance, they placed a drum in our rooms to bang to call for help.

On the last night of the safari, the camp hosted an amazing dinner for us under the stars. We were led down a winding path lined with luminaries and seated at a big long table next to a roaring bonfire. The ambiance was amazing. At a time like this, you realize that you are experiencing a once-in-a-lifetime moment. We could hear the animals out in the reserve as we gazed at the marvelous night sky. Local dancers and musicians performed for us by the light of the fire.

It truly was a perfect night. Perfect, that is, until one of the camp staff members interrupted our dessert. "Dinner is over. There is a lion in the camp!" We were instructed to head to our chalets immediately. The staff member further announced that chalets 7, 8, and 9, needed to be transported back to their rooms by armed guard because the lions were extremely close to those particular chalets. Of course, we were in chalet number 7. Apparently, the lions were unsuccessful hunting that day in the reserve, so they were still on the prowl. And they now had crossed over to our territory.

You can imagine the type of frenzy this situation could create. Instead, everyone tossed up a few "I hope they find you first" jokes and quickly returned to their chalets.

The next several hours were interesting to say the least. We could hear the lions circling. We could hear their roars as they communicated back and forth to one another, but we couldn't see anything outside of our screened windows because it was pitch black out. Did I mention that our chalet had large screen windows, which was not much of a barrier to the outside world? At that point, I was starting to understand why there was an emergency drum in our room.

You would have thought that this environment would have kept me up all night. You would have thought fear would have gripped my heart and robbed me of my last night sleeping in the reserve. You would have been wrong. Not this girl. I went to one of my go-to Scriptures and started declaring it over my husband, my daughter, and myself, along with those we were traveling with. I quickly fell fast asleep.

> *He will cover you with his feathers, and under his wings you will find refuge; his faithfulness will be your shield and rampart.*
> – Psalm 91:4

You see, I had no reason to fear because I was covered and protected. I knew that the Lord was always faithful, and because of that, I had nothing to fear. His faithfulness was my shield. It was my rampart. He is trustworthy. Don't misunderstand, danger surrounded us on all sides. In fact, when the sun came up the next morning, I was amazed at the damage we witnessed all around the camp.

The lions certainly had their fun. There was a downed tree torn to pieces right outside our chalet. And to make matters worse, we saw signs that some elephants and hippos also participated in the after-hours camp party, again right outside our door.

I need you to catch this next point. Like these actual lions in Malawi, "the devil prowls around like a roaring lion looking for someone to devour" (1 Peter 5:8). He is on the hunt, looking for prey. He is looking for vulnerabilities and weaknesses in your life so that he can pounce on you. Unfortunately, as Christians, we often don't realize that the lions are, in fact, in the camp. We think their roar is farther away and that we are safe. The truth is that the enemy is often in the camp, trying to cause havoc and destruction.

Do we need to be afraid? No. Do we need to be aware? Absolutely. We need to default to our go-to Scriptures. Psalm 91 is the perfect passage of Scripture to memorize so that when the devil does come knocking, you are armed and ready to fight with the Word of God. We need to remember how to fight. Declare those Scriptures. Believe it in faith. And then, go to sleep. 🖋

GOING DEEPER

1. Why does the devil need to play by God's rules? Does it make you feel safer knowing that everything, including the enemy, must obey the name of Jesus?

2. Looking at your prayer routine, what will you do differently knowing that you have authority in the name of Jesus?

3. In stormy seasons, why is it important to run to your Heavenly Father for intimacy, not just for protection?

4. 1 John 4:18 says that "perfect love drives out fear." How does knowing that God's love for you is perfect remove worry and fear for your future? Read 1 John 4:13-18 and reflect on the reliability of God's love for you.

5. There was a lion in the camp, and I slept like a baby, knowing that my God had me covered. How can you apply this same type of faith to your life as you feel the attacks of the enemy prowling around you?

She Is Fearless

You will not fear the terror of night,
nor the arrow that flies by day,
nor the pestilence that stalks in
the darkness, nor the plague
that destroys at midday.

–Psalm 91:5-6

Times are downright scary. The world's natural response is to react in fear, and to be honest, I don't blame them. Who knows what tomorrow might bring? There are rumors of war, threats of terrorism, mass shootings, possible pandemic outbreaks (again), the list goes on. Just watch the news. It will give you hundreds of reasons to panic. So why should a woman of God not fear during these tumultuous times? The psalmist clearly depicts the steadfast heart of a follower of God being fearless. How is that possible? Is it even realistic in this day and age?

The short answer is yes, but it is going to take some work. If you want to have a peace that surpasses all understanding, you must spend time dwelling with the Lord, allowing Him to pour into you, build you up, and strengthen you. A woman who spends time with her Heavenly Father knows that she is not alone, that God is with her always. Her heart is aligned with the Lord's heart, and she feels protected and at ease no matter what situations surround her.

Though an army besiege me, my heart will not fear; though war break out against me, even then I will be confident.

–Psalm 27:3

It's important to note that Psalm 91:5-6 never says that there will be no terror at night or arrows that fly by day or pestilence or plagues that cause mass destruction. It just says that you will not be afraid of any of these things. The psalmist is letting us know that a woman who dwells in the secret place of the Most High will have supernatural peace even when the things that legitimately evoke fear surround her. She is fearless. Not oblivious, just fearless.

She is fearless. Not oblivious, just fearless.

"You will hear of wars and rumors of wars, but see to it that you are not alarmed. Such things must happen, but the end is still to come."

–Matthew 24:6

Let me tell you what fear is. Fear is a liar. Fear magnifies the what ifs, the worst-case scenarios, and makes them feel like a reality. Fear causes panic, not caution. Fear is a silent killer that slowly steals your peace, joy, and hope. And yet, if you surveyed women today, Christian women included, a majority of them would say that they struggle with fear and anxiety. The Lord never intended for His people to live in bondage to fear. Whether it is a fear of flying, a fear of spiders, a fear of speaking in public, a fear of harm and sickness, or simply a fear of the unknown, we must remember that fear is from the devil, and it must bow to the name of Jesus. We can all have freedom from fear. All of us. Jesus set us free!

"So if the Son sets you free, you will be free indeed."
– John 8:36

Faith Is a Choice

As you are now aware, I am not secretive about my battle with fear. It was a tool that the enemy wanted to use against me to stop me from becoming who I am in Christ. I will always testify to the supernatural power from the Holy Spirit that helped set me free. When my daughter told me that Jesus himself walked with her down the corridor of the Venetian that dreaded day many years ago, I should have never feared again. I should have been like, "Praise You, Jesus, You are true, You are faithful, and You are always there." But instead, I unknowingly allowed the enemy to take position in my heart and my mind.

All of a sudden, a world of danger and despair, one that I used to feel safe in, now troubled me. It was like one day, I was living in peace and joy, and the next moment, all the things that could happen to me or my family became a crushing reality. The enemy wanted to torment me, rob me of my peace, and make me think that I was no longer safe. He distorted the promises of God and tried to replace them with fear-filled images and what-if scenarios. He highlighted every little thing that could go wrong, and I made it my focus. Honestly, I don't really think I truly understood just how bound I was until I was set free. I justified my fear as being a good parent and thus controlled every little thing that my kids did. This way, a repeat incident or something even worse could never happen again. What an exhausting standard to live under!

I'm going to be completely honest, those years were tough on me. But understand, I wasn't crippled in bed, unable to function, as some would like to believe battling with fear looks like. I was a young mom, doing her mom stuff, laughing with her kids, loving her husband, and serving God. But this spirit of fear would creep into my life to try to steal my joy. The enemy was smart enough to know how to target me. He knew my areas of weakness and knew exactly what buttons to push. I realized that living in fear wasn't the life that God wanted me to have, and yet I still battled it. Then, one day, I had enough. I was desperate to know the constant peace the Scriptures talked about—the peace talked about in Psalm 91. And I decided to surrender it all at the feet of Jesus.

I had an epiphany moment during my prayer time that day. I realized that faith isn't something we just naturally flow in. It's a choice we must make each day, just like choosing which shoes to wear—stilettos or sandals of peace. I wasn't going to wake up one morning and not have fear anymore. We are surrounded by fear triggers—turn on the news, read the newspaper, or hear about a dear friend who has just been diagnosed with cancer. No, I needed to reprogram my natural thought default setting to one that defaults to God's promises, not what if that happens to me. You are fearless, not because you don't have any fears, but because you choose to live above them. Faith is a choice!

You are fearless, not because you don't have any fears, but because you choose to live above them. Faith is a choice!

That seemed so simple, yet so freeing. How could it be a choice? I certainly wasn't choosing fear. I hated the way I felt in those moments. Trust me, I didn't want to feel that way. I realized, however, that I was allowing the enemy to cripple my thoughts by entertaining them. Pay close attention to this. Each time the enemy whispered in my ear, I had a choice. Instead of rebuking that lie immediately and taking it captive, as the Scriptures instruct us to do, I tried to dispute the lie through my natural reasoning.

Let me give you an example. I remember going for a routine physical where my doctor detected some nodules on my thyroid. Just to be safe, further testing through an ultrasound was needed. As you may know, nodules on your thyroid are pretty common for women, but the enemy tried to torment me with thoughts of cancer. Right then and there, I should have transitioned into spiritual warfare mode, declaring Scriptures and rebuking those lies. I, on the other hand, decided to go to the internet to look at statistics on the percentage of nodules that come back cancerous. They were low. But statistics don't give you peace. Only Jesus does! This natural tactic will fail every single time.

But statistics don't give you peace. Only Jesus does!

Spiritual battles are fought with spiritual weapons, not natural ones. I needed to literally choose where I let my mind go by the supernatural power of the Holy Spirit. Faith was indeed a choice that I had to make each day. I needed to take God at His Word. I had to fight the devil with Scripture. Jesus does this in Matthew 4 when He was tempted by the devil in the desert. When you read through this passage, you see that Satan tries to twist the very words of God to manipulate Jesus. Jesus simply defeats him by responding with, "It is written." He doesn't entertain any of the enemy's lies, nor does He try to fight him with a long, wordy response. He fights with Scripture because the Word holds POWER, and those very Scriptures hold the same power when we declare them too. Why should we think that we need to fight Satan any differently than Jesus did?

> *Then Jesus was led by the Spirit into the wilderness to be tempted by the devil. After fasting forty days and forty nights, he was hungry. The tempter came to him and said, "If you are the Son of God, tell these stones to become bread."*
>
> *Jesus answered, "It is written: 'Man shall not live on bread alone, but on every word that comes from the mouth of God.'"*
>
> *Then the devil took him to the holy city and had him stand on the highest point of the temple. "If you are the Son of God," he said, "throw yourself down. For it is written: 'He will command his angels concerning you, and they will lift you up in their hands, so that you will not strike your foot against a stone.'"*
>
> *Jesus answered him, "It is also written: 'Do not put the Lord your God to the test.'"*
>
> *Again, the devil took him to a very high mountain and showed him all the kingdoms of the world and their splendor. "All this I will give you," he said, "if you will bow down and worship me."*
>
> *Jesus said to him, "Away from me, Satan! For it is written: 'Worship the Lord your God, and serve him only.'"*
>
> *Then the devil left him, and angels came and attended him.*
>
> – Matthew 4:1-11

As a woman who has been a Christian most of her life and in ministry for nearly half of it, one thing I can assure you is that Satan is a liar. Scripture clearly says that "there is no truth in him" and that he is "the father of lies" (John 8:44). With that said, we can often fall prey to his lies if we aren't careful. It is not enough to simply know Satan's agenda. We must fight him with the truth found only in Scripture. Additionally, we cannot give the enemy an open door to enter. Put safeguards around your mind and protect what you think about, what you watch on TV, and who you hang around with. Are you giving the enemy a way to enter by what you are consuming?

Once you truly get a hold of the fact that God's promises are for all of us, that's when you can fight using these promises to dispute those lies of the enemy. And if you don't have any Scriptures in your tool belt, then you need to open up your Bible, find them, and memorize them. So, when the lies flood in—and they will—remember, you have the power "to take captive every thought and make it obedient to Christ" (2 Corinthians 10:5).

Now, we have already established that having faith doesn't shield you from difficult seasons. It just means that you know that you won't be walking through those seasons alone. Peace doesn't come only from being shielded from every hardship. We will all walk through difficult times. Had that ultrasound, and later, biopsy, shown cancer, my Jesus would have walked me through that season as well. His promises are still true. It's in these moments that we meditate and declare these powerful passages of Scripture.

*You will keep in perfect peace those whose minds
are steadfast, because they trust in you.*
–Isaiah 26:3

*Even though I walk through the darkest valley,
I will fear no evil, for you are with me.*
–Psalm 23:4

*I keep my eyes always on the Lᴏʀᴅ. With him
at my right hand, I will not be shaken.*
–Psalm 16:8

I can't emphasize enough how powerful Psalm 91 was for me during my battle. Honestly, there were days in my late twenties and early thirties where I thought that living with fear was just what moms do, that this was what the rest of my life would feel like. I believed that once you have kids, you'll never sleep a restful night again. Sound familiar? So many of us think this is a reality. This is another lie from the pit of hell. And thankfully, this is not true. I am living proof of that.

This Is What Freedom Feels Like

There I was in the middle of the Liwonde National Park in Malawi. I had just spent an incredible week in that country working with charity: water. I jumped out of a safari truck, walked across the animal occupied reserve, and hopped on a tiny propeller plane that was about to transfer me back to the city of Blantyre, Malawi. Our pilot took off right on that dirt field in the reserve, with baboons crossing our path. As we made our ascent, I looked out my window and witnessed all the beauty down below. Reflecting on all that our team just did, all that I got to experience that week, I began to get choked up. Tears literally streamed down my face as I soaked in the magnificent view.

I thought back to the Jessica of fifteen years ago. She would have never done any of this. She would have found reasons not to leave her son back home, 7,600 miles away in Boston, because he couldn't take time away from grad school (even though he was twenty-two years old). She would have never walked through the remote villages of Malawi, interacting with all those beautiful souls. She would have never slept in a camp with lions, elephants, hippos, and crocodiles surrounding her chalet. She would have never gotten on that small plane on that makeshift runway in the middle of an animal reserve. And how sad would that have been! I would have missed so much if I allowed the devil to continue to take occupancy in my thought life. And that's when I realized, this is what freedom feels like! Fear was no longer my master. It had no more control over me. It had been so long that, frankly, I forgot that was how I used to live. I am a different person now, totally transformed, free to walk out my calling and my purpose.

Time to Be Set Free

To every woman who is reading this book, if fear is something you struggle with, small scale or complete bondage, you need to understand that God doesn't want you to live like this any longer. There is freedom for you too. You need to latch onto this Scripture in Psalm 91, and claim it for your life. We are called to live by faith, not fear. The two are impossible roommates. One will have to go. What will you choose? How will you spend your life? Will you trust that God has your life in the palm of His hands, or will you live as a slave to the lies that the devil wants you to believe?

> *Our Lord is loving and longsuffering, but he won't allow his people to dwell in unbelief. You may have been tested time after time and now the time has come for you to make a decision. God wants faith that endures the ultimate test, a faith that won't allow anything to shake you from trust and confidence in his faithfulness.* —David Wilkerson [1]

Some of you are so comfortable living in fear, that the thought of getting set free is more unsettling than changing. I get it—change is hard. Maybe some of you are older in years and figure that there is no point now. You might as well just live out the rest of your days as is. You've missed your window of opportunity. That is nonsense! As long as you woke up this morning and have breath in your lungs, God has a purpose and a plan for your life. You need to stop justifying and rationalizing this fear and deeming it acceptable.

It is also important to note that fear can be passed down from generation to generation. Watching one or both of your parents react in fear as a child will certainly program you to do the same as you develop. It's how you have been trained to cope with trying situations. Furthermore, there is a spiritual component here. If fear is something that is prevalent in your family line, there could be a generational stronghold that needs to be broken. Simply put, a generational stronghold is a sin or tendency not to trust God that is practiced over and over again until it becomes a habit. This habit (or stronghold) is then passed down to the next generation, creating a greater propensity with each passing generation.

The good news is that this battle isn't hopeless for those who have a relationship with Jesus. It was already won at the cross. We simply need to lay it down, repent, and walk in the freedom Christ gave us. If you don't want to fight this battle for yourself, do it for the next generation.

Let's pray this prayer together right now.

Dear Jesus,

Thank You for dying on the cross for my sins. Thank You for the freedom that You generously give. First, I ask You right now to forgive me for my fear, control, and doubt when it comes to trusting You and Your plan for my life. I lay it all down at Your feet. Secondly, I break off any generational stronghold in this area of my life and boldly walk in the freedom that You so richly offer. When old tendencies start to creep in, remind me that I am no longer a slave to fear, but a daughter set free to chase after all that You have in store. Keep my mind set on Your Holy Scriptures to direct each step of my life.

In Jesus's precious name. Amen.

GOING DEEPER

1. Matthew 24:6 states that wars and such things must happen. How does the world respond? How should you respond as a child of God?

2. What fears are trying to take a hold of you today? How are you responding? Try to distinguish between concern (legitimate) and worry (unfounded).

3. Control is often the gut reaction to being afraid. We need to recognize that control is just another tool the enemy uses to take our trust away from God and then put it in ourselves. In what areas have you replaced fear with a spirit of control?

4. "Statistics don't give you peace, only Jesus does." How does this statement challenge your current tactics for dealing with bad news or tenuous situations?

5. Jesus fought Satan by quoting Scripture. Do you believe that the Scriptures are as powerful in your mouth as they were in Jesus's?

6. Is there a generational pattern of fear in your life? Can you identify any strongholds that may have been established in your family line? If so, pray a prayer of freedom to be set free once and for all.

She Watches from Afar

A thousand may fall at your side,
ten thousand at your right hand,
but it will not come near you. You
will only observe with your eyes and
see the punishment of the wicked.

–Psalm 91:7-8

There was wailing in all of Egypt that dreadful night. The cries, screams, and desperate moans from heartbroken family members bellowed in the midnight air. The Egyptians had already suffered a great deal due to the nine other plagues that ripped through their land, but Pharaoh's heart was hardened, and he wouldn't relent. Plague after plague struck the land of Egypt—boils, locusts, hail, frogs, and more—and yet Pharaoh still refused to let the Israelites go.

> *"Therefore, say to the Israelites: 'I am the L*ORD*,*
> *and I will bring you out from under the yoke of the*
> *Egyptians. I will free you from being slaves to them,*
> *and I will redeem you with an outstretched arm and*
> *with mighty acts of judgment.'"*
> – Exodus 6:6

The people of Israel had cried out year after year, petitioning God for mercy to free them from the yoke of slavery that was upon them for 430 years. The Lord had had enough and would hold back his anger no longer. He sent the Angel of Death to pass over Egypt, killing the firstborn of both man and animal alike. The angel's instructions were simple: kill the firstborn in each household, unless the top of the doorframes of the household were anointed with the blood of a spotless, sacrificial lamb (Exodus 12:7). Those were the instructions God gave to the Israelites, to His people. This blood foreshadowed the blood Jesus Christ would shed on the cross over fifteen hundred years later, breaking the curse of sin and death over His people once and for all. Although no exact numbers are recorded in the history book, theologians estimate around one hundred thousand to two hundred thousand people plus livestock died that night.[1]

> *So Moses said, "This is what the L*ORD *says: 'About*
> *midnight I will go throughout Egypt. Every firstborn*
> *son in Egypt will die, from the firstborn son of Pharaoh,*

who sits on the throne, to the firstborn son of the female
slave, who is at her hand mill, and all the firstborn of
the cattle as well. There will be loud wailing throughout
Egypt—worse than there has ever been or ever will be
again. But among the Israelites not a dog will bark at
any person or animal.' Then you will know that the LORD
makes a distinction between Egypt and Israel."
– Exodus 11:4-7

The Lord makes a distinction between His people and those who are not. I just love that. Our Heavenly Father holds a distinction in His heart, providing special protection for His children. Although hundreds of thousands of Egyptians suffered death at the hand of the Lord, the Angel of Death did not come near the Israelites who obediently applied the blood of the lamb to their door frames. They were spared. But the Egyptians and their false gods could not save themselves from this fate. The Israelites had been set apart (Deuteronomy 14:2). The same promise and assurance are true for us.

Safe from the Punishment of the Wicked

As one who has made God her refuge, who runs to Him instead of the world, I am safe. Knowing that, I can confidently hang on to this verse in Psalm 91 no matter what turmoil and strife surround me. "A thousand may fall at [my] side, ten thousand at [my] right" (Psalm 91:7). I need not fear because I am marked as His. A distinction has been made in the spirit world.

At first glance, the Scripture might make the reader believe that no danger or death will ever come near you as you sit by and just watch. This is not the intention of the verse. If you read it carefully, you will see that the heart of this verse is focused on the "it." The "it" is very significant. What won't come near you? "It" won't come near you. The "it" is the punishment of the wicked.

The psalmist is assuring us that, as children of God, we need not fear His punishment or wrath. This Scripture is not talking about general protection from the normal dangers that this world presents. This Scripture is solely about the protection we receive from the punishment or judgment extended to those who walk in direct disobedience to God's ways. The Amplified Version makes it a little clearer to understand.

You will only [be a spectator as you] look on with your eyes and witness the [divine] repayment of the wicked [as you watch safely from the shelter of the Most High].
– Psalm 91:8 (AMP)

A woman who dwells with Him watches from afar and sees the punishment of the wicked. She sees what penalty comes with disobedience. She witnesses the consequences of those who despise the Lord and worship idols and gods before Him. A woman who makes God her Most High, who knows whose she is, who doesn't prioritize anything above Him, can walk confidently through the devastation unscathed. She observes His power all around her and doesn't fear because she is confident in who she serves. That dreadful night in Egypt, darkness and death were all around, but it did not come near God's people. They only observed the punishment with their eyes.

The Egyptians were downright horrible to the Israelites, working them without mercy, treating them like animals and property. They were ruthless, inflicting suffering and unthinkable hardships on them. Watching from afar, hearing the cries and moans of the Egyptians must have been difficult to listen to. And yet, at the same time, it was the sound of judgment for those who mocked the Lord Almighty and vindication for His chosen people.

This event in the Old Testament really speaks of the character of God! God will not be mocked. Nor will He allow His people to be mistreated. God wanted to release the Israelites from the oppression they endured so that He could begin to build the nation of Israel as He promised Abraham (Genesis 17:6). God is holy, and because He is holy, He will not tolerate sin, disobedience, or mistreatment of His people. He is a patient and loving God, but judgment will come to those who live in rebellion to His ways. We cannot forget that. "The LORD is slow to anger but great in power; the LORD will not leave the guilty unpunished" (Nahum 1:3). That is the very essence of who He is. And, furthermore, God's timing, not ours, is perfect.

I will punish the world for its evil, the wicked for their sins. I will put an end to the arrogance of the haughty and will humble the pride of the ruthless.
–Isaiah 13:11

The assurance of safety and protection found in Psalm 91:7-8 is for those who make the Most High their dwelling place, those who find refuge and strength in God, and those New Testament Christians who have received Jesus Christ as their personal Lord and Savior. These individuals do not need to fear the punishment that comes for the wicked because they are marked as children of God.

We do, however, live in a fallen world full of sin. War, natural disasters, pandemics, and pure acts of evil are on display daily. Bad things happen. But God is in control, and we need not fear, no matter what transpires. We need to keep our eyes on the Lord and remember that God is in control.

It's Always Been about the Blood

As powerful as Psalm 91:7-8 are in comforting God's chosen people today, I believe that these verses also hold a prophetic message for future days to come. One day, we will all stand before Jesus face to face. Scripture tells us so. We will be accountable for all of our words, actions, motives, and thoughts as they will be on full display before Him. Once again, there will be a distinction made between those who are His and those who are not. Make no mistake, we will all have to give an account for the things we did as we lived our life on earth. However, despite all of our failures and shortcomings, if we have accepted Jesus Christ's free gift of salvation and apply the blood of Jesus over our lives, our slate will be wiped clean, and we will spend eternity in Heaven with Him.

For we must all appear before the judgment seat
of Christ, so that each of us may receive what

is due us for the things done while in the body,
whether good or bad.
– 2 Corinthians 5:10

Sin entered the world through Adam and Eve. God's plan for us was to live in obedience, dwell with Him, and take care of the earth He gifted us. It was simple. But Satan deceived Adam and Eve, and sin manifested. Everything changed. Humanity now had a propensity to sin, separating us all from God. The Bible is clear on the penalty for sin—it's death!

For the wages of sin is death, but the gift of God
is eternal life in Christ Jesus our Lord.
– Romans 6:23

Thankfully, God did not give up on us. He desired to spend eternity with us. So out of His great and intense love, He sent His one and only son Jesus to earth to pay the penalty for our sin once and for all. Jesus shed His precious blood on the cross so that we may be forgiven. He paid a debt He didn't owe so that we could be reconciled to the Father. All of our missteps, ugliness, shameful deeds, and pride, all of it is washed away by His blood. There is no sin too big, no deed too

All of our missteps, ugliness, shameful deeds, and pride, all of it is washed away by His blood.

shocking that the blood of Jesus can't wipe away. Whether it is idolatry, selfishness, adultery, stealing, gossip, greed, strife, drunkenness, rebellion, perversion, sexual impurity, witchcraft, disobedience, profanity, jealousy, lying, or murder, it is covered by the blood. All we need to do is receive this precious gift in faith.

It's always been about the blood! That's what separates us. That dreadful night in Egypt, it was the blood of the sacrificed lamb that set the Israelites apart. Today, it is the blood of Jesus Christ that sets us apart. In both instances, it's all in the application of the blood. I believe that had an Israelite refused to obey God's command to apply the blood to the doorframes, he would have experienced the same fate as the Egyptians. If we don't receive Jesus's sacrifice on the cross, our fate is also sealed. We are redeemed by the blood of Jesus Christ. There is no covering for those who don't receive it.

The blood will be a sign for you on the houses where you are, and when I see the blood, I will pass over you. No destructive plague will touch you when I strike Egypt.
–Exodus 12:13

In him we have redemption through his blood, the forgiveness of sins, in accordance with the riches of God's grace.
–Ephesians 1:7

"He himself bore our sins" in his body on the cross, so that we might die to sins and live for righteousness; "by his wounds you have been healed."
–1 Peter 2:24

*Surely he took up our pain and bore our suffering,
yet we considered him punished by God, stricken
by him, and afflicted. But he was pierced for our
transgressions, he was crushed for our iniquities;
the punishment that brought us peace was on him,
and by his wounds we are healed.*

–Isaiah 53:4-5

God voluntarily sacrificed His Son for us. God loves us so much that He allowed His Son to be brutally beaten and receive a criminal's death on the cross in order to atone for all the sins we have committed. Blood had to be shed. In the Old Testament, a spotless lamb was killed and the sins of that person were placed on the innocent lamb. One life for another. But thankfully, Jesus is the last and final sacrifice. No more animal sacrifices are needed because His life paid it all for each one of us.

But You Need to Take the First Step

I sometimes get so overwhelmed by the love of the Father that it is hard for me to even comprehend the magnitude of that sacrifice. I'm not deserving, none of us are, and yet He loved us despite our unworthiness. If you have not invited Jesus into your life, if you have not received the gift of salvation through Jesus Christ, then now is your opportunity. Please pray with me.

Dear Jesus,

Thank You for dying on the cross for me. I believe You died and rose again, paying my debt in full. I confess all my sins before You, known and unknown, and ask for Your forgiveness. Help me to live a life that honors You by the equipping power of the Holy Spirit. I lay down all my efforts and control and invite You into my heart to be Lord and Savior. In Jesus's precious name. Amen.

If you have said that prayer, whether it was the first time praying it or you prayed it forty years ago, you have assurance that you are His. You've been redeemed and are set apart as a child of God. All the promises given in this psalm and throughout Scripture are for you, as you faithfully walk out your life safe from the traps of the enemy. There is a distinction made between you and the world. For those who make Jesus their Most High and have received His gift of salvation, you need not fear the punishment of the wicked. They will be winnowed out like chaff and burned in the fire. "A thousand may fall at your side, ten thousand at your right hand, but [in that day of judgment] it will not come near you" (Psalm 91:7). 🕊

"As the weeds are pulled up and burned in the fire, so it will be at the end of the age. The Son of Man will send out his angels, and they will weed out of his kingdom everything that causes sin and all who do evil. They will throw them into the blazing furnace, where there will be weeping and gnashing of teeth. Then the righteous will shine like the sun in the kingdom of their Father. Whoever has ears, let them hear."

–Matthew 13:40-43

GOING DEEPER

1. How does it make you feel knowing that a distinction has been made between being a child of God and those who do not know Him?

2. God will not be mocked! In a world full of blatant disobedience and disregard for the things of God, why is God still slow to bring judgment on those people?

3. The blood placed on the Israelites' door frames in Egypt was a foreshadowing of the blood Jesus would shed on the cross. Do you agree that, had the Israelites refused to mark their door frames, the Angel of Death would have struck the firstborn child in their household? What will happen to those who refuse to accept Jesus's sacrifice on the cross?

She Declares

If you say, "The LORD is my refuge,"
and you make the Most High
your dwelling, no harm will
overtake you, no disaster will
come near your tent.

–Psalm 91:9-10

This Scripture, right here, is probably the one I quote and pray the most often. It gives me such assurance each and every day as I speak this over my family. I have great confidence in my loving Father who wants to protect me and keep me safe. But it is important to note that the promises of safety and security follow an if-then format, meaning that it is, in fact, conditional. The psalmist clearly states that "if you say" and "you make," then "no harm will overtake you, no disaster will come near your tent." Pay careful attention to the sentence structure.

We all want the benefits and blessings of safety that God provides; however, we must decide in our hearts that He is in fact the one we make our refuge.

God doesn't want 90 percent of your heart. He doesn't. He wants it all. He is a loving, generous God, but He is also a jealous God who doesn't want to share you with the things that occupy your heart. I often hear this parallel to marriage, and it truly drives this point home. Imagine if your husband came home one day and said to you, "You are my everything. I love you so much, but about ten percent of the time, I am going to be with other women. But please know I love you most." Well, I don't know about you, but that wouldn't work for me. And sweet friend, I pray that is not acceptable for your marriage either.

> *He is a loving, generous God, but He is also a jealous God who doesn't want to share you with the things that occupy your heart.*

When you are in a committed relationship, it's exclusive. I am either enough for my husband, or I am not, but there is no sharing allowed in my marriage. He can sing me love songs. He can give me extravagant gifts. He can hold my hand. He can write me the most beautiful love letters. But if someone else is occupying 10 percent of his attention, or even 1 percent for that matter, we would be done. All of those acts would mean nothing to me. Our Heavenly Father feels the same way about us! He wants to be your everything.

Making Him Lord

We need to remember that God isn't just our Savior and Protector, as some would like to believe, He is also our Lord. A lord is "a person who has authority, control, or power over others."[1] Lord means ruler. And that is exactly the role God should have in our lives. Being your Lord does not mean that He is some magical genie-in-a-bottle character who grants your every wish and desire. Making Him Lord doesn't just mean we run to Him when we get ourselves into a pickle or when life takes a turn that we did not expect. Making Him Lord means that He is in charge, and we obey. We are to submit to our Heavenly Father daily, seek His counsel, follow His instructions faithfully, and make Him our dwelling.

We read through this passage of Scripture so quickly sometimes that we neglect to focus on the heart of the message from the psalmist. This is a beautiful promise, but it is for those who make Him their refuge. Too often, I watch Christians walk through struggle after struggle after struggle, shrugging their shoulders, wondering why God has forsaken them. They wonder where He is in the midst of their disaster, blaming the Lord for having a deaf ear to their cries for help. This couldn't be farther from the truth.

Often times, it's our actions that are preventing God from moving. We may go to church, sing the songs, and say all the right Christian phrases, but if we fail to give God the full surrender He so richly desires, we block Him from moving in our lives. He is looking for our actions to support our declaration that He is indeed our Most High.

What does this mean exactly? It means that we diligently and faithfully read the Bible, looking for correction, instruction, and guidance, and we intentionally put into practice what we learn. It means doing the hard stuff and holding the unpopular stance, even when no one else is doing it or when culture tells you otherwise because it pleases God. It means running to the Father's feet when life's uncertainties hit us, rather than seeking counsel from worldly systems, the internet, our friends and family, or anything else that tries to become a poor substitute to the Creator of the universe.

Where Do You Run?

We are called to be different. Scripture says we are strangers (1 Peter 2:11) in this world, which means we may appear strange to those who don't know the Lord like we do. If people are surprised when you tell them that you are a Christian, then you are doing something wrong. The way you treat people (to their faces and behind their backs) should be laced with love and compassion like Jesus demonstrated. The language we use, the conversations we engage in, the things we avoid, and even the entertainment we watch and listen to should not compromise who we are as children of God. And most importantly, where you find your strength and refuge should only be in God Most High. Then and only then can we declare these Scriptures with confidence.

Where do you run when the bank account is low? Who do you call upon when you are sick or depressed or lonely? In what do you put your confidence in when the world around you shakes and fear is trying to rise up? It should be our Heavenly Father. And yet, we try to use other people or things to give us security that only He can provide.

Your spouse is one of the greatest gifts God can bless you with. He is your sounding board, your prayer partner, and the one you get to do life with, but he cannot be your refuge.

Going to your doctor for routine appointments and check-ups is so important, but at the end of the day, these tests will not prevent you from sickness and disease. Trust me, I learned this firsthand. Finding refuge in doctors will only give you temporary relief until the next health issue arises. Instead, run to God to give you good health.

Similarly, following the latest health craze, eating a nutrient-rich diet, and exercising regularly are valuable habits to incorporate into your daily living. I highly encourage them. But your faith can't rest in these lifestyle choices. They will not guarantee you a long life, nor can they be the thing that you make your refuge.

You can't make money, your job, social status, success, your education, your natural talent, gifting, or self-help techniques your refuge. As we covered in chapter 3, refuge is the person or place you run to for protection. Stop defaulting to the things of this world. This role can't be filled by anyone or anything but our Heavenly Father. And when we make this declaration and live a life that runs to the Father first, He shields us from the disasters that surround us.

> *When we live our lives within the shadow of God*
> *Most High, our secret hiding place, we will always*
> *be shielded from harm. How then could evil prevail*
> *against us or disease infect us?*
> – Psalm 91:9-10 (TPT)

Don't you just love how this Scripture reads from the Passion Translation? What an amazing God we serve! He promises us that if we simply make Him first, He will guard us from all harm—the demonic forces of evil and the diseases that surround us. But He has to be the place we run to.

I think many of us need to renounce the false refuges we have created in our lives. We have elevated systems and people above our Heavenly Father. No matter what life throws at us, He desires for us to turn toward Him with an undivided heart. He wants to be the place we run to when life's difficulties arise. Cry out to Him alone while you sit at His feet. Let His presence minister to your soul. Feed your spirit with the truth found all throughout the Scriptures. Reflect on His character and His promises.

God Does Not Change!

Every good and perfect gift is from above, coming
down from the Father of the heavenly lights, who
does not change like shifting shadows.

–James 1:17

God Is Just!

"And the heavens proclaim his righteousness,
for he is a God of justice."

–Psalm 50:6

God Is Gracious, Righteous,
and Compassionate!

The LORD is gracious and righteous;
our God is full of compassion.

–Psalm 116:5

God Is Jealous!

For the LORD your God is a consuming fire, a jealous God.

–Deuteronomy 4:24

God's Love Is Limitless and He Is Faithful!

Your love, LORD, reaches to the heavens,
your faithfulness to the skies.

–Psalm 36:5

God Is Our Strength and Helper!

God is our refuge and strength,
an ever-present help in trouble.

–Psalm 46:1

God Is Trustworthy!
Trust in the Lord forever, for the Lord,
the Lord himself, is the Rock eternal.

– Isaiah 26:4

David Knew Who to Take Refuge in

Did you know that some scholars believe that King David either authored Psalm 91 or modified it, with Moses potentially being the original author? In either instance, it is clear throughout Scripture that King David understood the truth of making the Most High his dwelling. David's life was marked with many victories and triumphs. However, much of it was full of trials and hardships. Knowing where to turn and who to take refuge in helped David become the powerful king he was, while evading death and disaster numerous times.

Before King David assumed the throne, King Saul pursued David relentlessly, trying to kill him. David was innocent, but that didn't stop Saul. Rooted in jealousy and demonic lies, he had resolved in his heart to end David's life. He became obsessed with this. But David never lost faith in God. In fact, during this season, David wrote many of the Psalms. Psalm 57 is one David penned as he was hiding in the craggy rocks of Ein Gedi, trying to avoid King Saul's wrath.

Have mercy on me, my God, have mercy on me, for in
you I take refuge. I will take refuge in the shadow of
your wings until the disaster has passed.

– Psalm 57:1

David didn't take refuge in military strategy. He didn't take refuge in his close circle of confidants either. As David had done his entire life, he took refuge in the one and only God. Did spending time with God help him with his military strategy? Yes. Did it also help him know who he could trust? Absolutely. But it was God and God alone that David made his dwelling. And this is what kept him safe as disaster passed by him. We must do the same if we don't want disaster to come near us.

No Disaster Will Come Near Your Tent

Back in biblical times, the Israelites lived in tents made from long pieces of goatshair cloth about five to six feet in length, which were attached to a series of wooden poles that were hammered into the ground. There wasn't much to it, but that's where they lived. We have certainly come a long way. Our homes may vary in size and style, but most homes these days provide a secure roof, protective walls, and running water. We no longer live a Bedouin lifestyle; however, the Scripture remains steadfast and holds the same promise of protection for our tents (homes) today.

A few years ago, A tornado ripped through my small town. For those of you who aren't familiar with Connecticut, this is totally abnormal. We get our fair share of ice storms, blizzards, nor'easters and even the occasional hurricane, but tornados aren't typical in this area. And on the off chance that one forms, it is so minor that barely any damage occurs. This was not the case in May of 2018.

I honestly will remember this day forever, as I had never experienced something like this before. My son had youth group that night, and weather forecasts were predicting some pretty heavy storms ripping through the area. This in itself was not unusual. Although my son was seventeen and had his license for over a year, I decided I would drive him to church that night, just to be cautious. We were just heading to the car when an alert went off on my phone, signaling us to take cover because tornados were in the area. Thankfully, I've watched a lot of movies and television shows where this has happened, so I knew exactly what to do.

I grabbed a flashlight and told both my kids (and dog) to head straight to the basement. To be honest, I began to doubt that we were actually under a real threat because the skies seemed just a little overcast. I stood at the top of our basement stairs, peering out a nearby window to see if something would actually transpire. Then it did. The skies quickly turned from overcast to pitch black in a matter of minutes. A sound similar to a freight train announced that something bad was headed our way. Winds were whipping about, debris started flying, and then all visibility was lost. At that point, I high-tailed it back down to the basement, joined my kids, and began to pray this very verse in Psalm 91.

Oh Lord,

You promised that no harm would befall us and that no disaster would come near our tent. I pray right now that not a tree in our yard or any flying object would hit our home. Surround us, our property, and this house with your warring angels. Put a hedge of protection around us and keep us safe!

In Jesus's precious name. Amen!

You see, this Scripture and promise was so deeply embedded in my heart that, when disaster was headed our way, I knew exactly how to pray, and I knew exactly who to run to. I knew we would be safe because I ran to the Most High, and I knew He would be faithful. And He was. That is why it is important to know the character and promises of God. It is crucial in these moments.

Destruction surrounded us on every side. The damage in our town was indescribable. Houses were destroyed. Trees blocked roadways for days. The power was out for over a week in most areas, including our house. But we were safe, and our "tent" was untouched. I think we only had a couple of small branches down in our yard and some leaves scattered about. This was not the story for the homeowners just one street over from us. They were directly hit by this tornado.

I take these Scriptures very seriously. I have memorized them, studied them,

> I've learned time and time again that it's what's done in the quiet that prepares you for the challenging moments in your life.

and have written them on the tablet of my heart. I've learned time and time again that it's what's done in the quiet that prepares you for the challenging moments in your life. Ladies, we need to learn to dwell with Him when things are good so that we are prepared when things are not. God wants us to run to Him as a child runs to his father when things get scary. But God also wants us to run to Him when things are good so that we can be built up in His strength to take on all that may come our way. God is our refuge! ✍

GOING DEEPER

1. As you examine your life, what have you been making your refuge? Are there areas of your heart that are divided?

2. What areas do you think Christians compromise the most in? Why do you think they are able to justify this behavior?

3. David's devotion was tested many times, yet he remained faithful to God Most High. Although David also made some major mistakes along the way (Bathsheba and Absalom, to name a few), God still considered him "a man after his own heart" (1 Sam 13:14; Acts 13:22). Why do you think this is the case?

4. Why is it so important to have Scripture memorized? What are your favorite go-to Scriptures?

5. "It's what's done in the quiet that prepares you for the challenging moments in your life." What does this statement mean to you? What areas do you need to spend more time focusing on during your quiet time with the Lord?

She Is Surrounded

For he will command his angels
concerning you to guard you in all
your ways; they will lift you up in
their hands, so that you will not
strike your foot against a stone.
You will tread on the lion and the
cobra; you will trample the great
lion and the serpent.

–Psalm 91:11-13

So many of us go about our daily lives looking at what
transpires only with natural eyes. We see things con-
cretely and neglect to recognize that there is a spirit world

all around us where battles are taking place moment by moment. When God promises to command His angels concerning us, He unleashes an army in the spirit world to surround us and keep us from harm. If we could just get one glimpse into the spiritual world, we would be astonished to see a mighty army surrounding us, fighting on our behalf.

Doesn't that bring you such peace, knowing that the Angel Armies are on assignment to protect you and defend you throughout your lifetime? I often take for granted this protection that the Lord so richly offers. I sometimes lay awake at night wondering how often an angel had to intercede on my behalf that day. Knowing me, it's probably a lot. I'm guessing I have likely been labeled "a real handful" in the Heavenlies.

But really, have you ever thought about that? Have you ever driven by a bad car accident and thought, if I had just left the house two minutes earlier, that could have been me? Or have you almost taken a bad fall on the ice and then suddenly regained your balance? Was that you, or was there an angel holding you up so that you wouldn't fall?

Several years ago, my family and I were headed up north for some skiing. Weather forecasts were predicting loads of snow, so it was an optimal time to drive up. We all piled into the car, and off we went. But to our surprise, the storm arrived earlier than expected and in the form of ice, not snow, as originally forecasted. We weren't sure what to do. Should we turn around and drive back through the ice, or should we keep going forward, hoping that this skating rink of a highway would soon transition into snow as we got further north?

Even though we were driving at a snail's pace, our car was still slipping and sliding all over the highway. As we continued on our course, I saw brake lights in front of us and cars spinning out of control as we approached an overpass. Bracing for the worst, I quickly realized we were about to become part of a multi-car accident. Our car had now also begun to spin out of control. I could see cars crashing—one into another into another. The sound of cars clanking into each other resounded in that cold night air. I shouted out, "Jesus, protect us," and soon thereafter, our car came to a halting stop. It was over. Or so I thought, the cars behind us were swerving, now headed straight for us. Boom! Our car rocked with force and moved forward several feet.

Deep breath in, deep breath out. Besides some nervous kids in the backseat, thankfully, we were all safe. Now to survey the damage to the car. To our great surprise, our car remained untouched through it all. Miraculously, and I don't say that lightly, our car did not get hit, even though we felt a large bump after we came to a stop. I believe an angel literally moved our car out of the line of fire and prevented us from getting hit. Our car had absolutely no damage, not even a scratch, and none of us were injured. And yet, all around us was the wreckage of at least twenty cars in a massive pile-up. We slowly weaved our way off the overpass, in between the damaged vehicles, and continued on our way.

Not for one moment do I take for granted what happened to us that night. When Scripture says, "He will command His angels concerning you to guard you in all of your ways" (Psalm 91:11), it is true and reliable. As I mentioned earlier, praying Psalm 91 over me and my family had become a daily part of my time with the Lord. I recognized the power that this love letter from God possessed, and in faith, I received it and proclaimed it each and every day.

In the midst of our car spin-out, there was no time for me to start reciting full Scriptures. I could barely speak, "Jesus, protect us." It all happened so quickly. But that morning, when I prayed, "They will lift you up so that your foot will not strike a stone," God heard and sent His angels out on assignment. In our case, I believe that the angels picked up our car and moved us out of the hit zone, shielding us from a dangerous accident. We remained untouched.

Another time, I remember my mother and I were driving back from an evening outlet shopping trip. I was newly married, and it was so nice to meet up with my mother for a night out. As we were driving home, I was so engaged in the conversation that I accidentally got off at the wrong exit. Immediately, I knew I had made a horrible mistake and was now driving in an extremely unsafe area. Did I mention we were completely lost too? We began to pray, and out of nowhere, a police officer showed up. I vividly remember the look of panic on his face when he approached our car as we were stopped at a traffic light. Confused as to why two women were alone at night driving in one of the most dangerous neighborhoods in this city, he instructed us to keep driving, not to stop for any reason (even at stop signs or traffic lights), and gave us directions back to the highway.

I truly believe God positioned that police officer at that intersection for our protection and direction. I wouldn't be surprised if it was an angel on assignment. And furthermore, I believe that there were angels surrounding my car as we drove in this crime-stricken area of the city. I can only imagine the kind of fate we could have endured without the Almighty's protection. What if someone decided to carjack my vehicle or pulled a gun on us or even worse? But God's promises are true. We were surrounded.

Commanded Angels

The Word of God promises us that "He will command His angels concerning us in all our ways" (Psalm 91:11). I love that part, "in all our ways." He will protect us in every situation. Not some, but all—in our coming and our going, in our lying down and our rising up. Even when our ways are careless mistakes (and we take the wrong exit off the highway), He will protect us.

The famous evangelist Billy Graham wrote a book in 1986 titled *Angels, God's Secret Agents*. The book highlights true stories of God's provision, where He dispatched angels on assignment to protect His people. One story in particular really made me take pause and reflect on the protection we truly have in the spirit world. It makes Psalm 91 come to life.

John Paton was a missionary in the New Hebrides islands. One night the warriors from one of the local tribes surrounded the mission headquarters, planning to burn the Patons out and kill them. As you can imagine, John Paton and his wife were terrified, and prayed all through the night that God would save them. When daylight came they were astonished to see the warriors leave without attacking them.

A year later the chief of the tribe became a Christian. During the course of their conversations John Paton asked the chief about that night. What had kept the warriors from burning down the house and killing them? The chief answered this question with a question of his own, "Who were all those men you had there with you?" Paton replied, "There was no one other than my wife and I." The chief strongly disagreed. He told Paton that he and his warriors had seen hundreds of men standing guard around the mission headquarters, men with shining clothes, holding drawn swords.[1]

Being surrounded by God's Angel Armies is threaded throughout Scripture. We read many accounts of angels actively interceding on behalf of God's people. Let's look at Daniel's life. We can't dismiss the angel activity found in this book as mere children's stories, as some would like to do. This is an account of the marvelous power of God Most High discharging His angels on Daniel's behalf.

Daniel refused to stop praying to God even though King Nebuchadnezzar's edict had dire consequences.

Anyone caught praying to anyone but the king would be sent to the lions' den, which ultimately resulted in a horrific death—being torn limb by limb by a ravenous beast. This proclamation didn't stop Daniel from praying. He feared God more than anything that mere man could sentence him to and proceeded to go back to his room to pray each day. Who knows, maybe one of Daniel's prayers might have been the recitation of this portion of Scripture found in Psalm 91. Despite the king's admiration for Daniel, the decree stood.

> *So the king gave the order, and they brought*
> *Daniel and threw him into the lions' den.*
> *The king said to Daniel, "May your God, whom*
> *you serve continually, rescue you!"*
> – Daniel 6:16

Daniel was thrown into the den, and the stone was placed in front of it, locking him in for certain death. But as the king hoped, God Almighty, whom David served, saved Daniel. Those hungry lions didn't stand a chance against the angels God commanded to watch over Daniel. What power! What authority! What assurance we have in God our father!

> *"My God sent his angel, and he shut the mouths of*
> *the lions. They have not hurt me, because I was found*
> *innocent in his sight. Nor have I ever done any wrong*
> *before you, Your Majesty."*
> – Daniel 6:22

You will tread on the lion and the cobra; you will
trample the great lion and the serpent.
–Psalm 91:13

Rescuing Lot from ultimate destruction is another example in Scripture of God sending His angels to protect us. Lot was living in a depraved land. Sin was rampant. All types of debauchery and perversion were taking place in Sodom and Gomorrah. The people who lived there had turned their hearts away from the things of God and lost all shame. The things people were involved in were unthinkable. Lot and his family, unfortunately, had grown quite comfortable in this God-forsaken land. Even though Abraham interceded on behalf of his nephew and his family, God's wrath of destruction was inevitable for Sodom and Gomorrah.

But God was faithful to Abraham's plea and sent an angel to rescue Lot and his family.

With the coming of dawn, the angels urged Lot,
saying, "Hurry! Take your wife and your two
daughters who are here, or you will be swept away
when the city is punished."
–Genesis 19:15

Heeding the Warnings

An angel was on assignment to watch over Lot and his family. But we must heed the warnings that God sends. Lot's two sons-in-laws thought the warning was a joke and refused to leave and thus sealed their fate. And although instructed not to look back, Lot's wife turned into "a pillar of salt" (Genesis 19:26). She refused to obey God's command and looked back at her comfortable, sin-filled life with fondness. And with that hesitation, she too was annihilated.

What would have happened if Lot refused to go? I believe that he too would have been destroyed. It is important that we are constantly listening to God's direction for our lives. We want all the protection He so generously offers in Psalm 91, but if we fail to do our part and obey, then we reject the very protection we so greatly desire. This reminds me of the story of the Drowning Man.

A terrible storm came into a town and local officials sent out an emergency warning that the riverbanks would soon overflow and flood the nearby homes. They ordered everyone in the town to evacuate immediately.

A faithful Christian man heard the warning and decided to stay, saying to himself, "I will trust God and if I am in danger, then God will send a divine miracle to save me."

The neighbors came by his house and said to him, "We're leaving and there is room for you in our car, please come with us!" But the man declined. "I have faith that God will save me."

As the man stood on his porch watching the water rise up the steps, a man in a canoe paddled by and called to him, "Hurry and come into my canoe, the waters are rising quickly!" But the man again said, "No thanks, God will save me."

The floodwaters rose higher pouring water into his living room and the man had to retreat to the second floor. A police motorboat came by and saw him at the window. "We will come up and rescue you!" they shouted. But the man refused, waving them off saying, "Use your time to save someone else! I have faith that God will save me!"

The flood waters rose higher and higher and the man had to climb up to his rooftop.

A helicopter spotted him and dropped a rope ladder. A rescue officer came down the ladder and pleaded with the man, "Grab my hand and I will pull you up!" But the man STILL refused, folding his arms tightly to his body. "No thank you! God will save me!"

Shortly after, the house broke up and the floodwaters swept the man away and he drowned.

When in Heaven, the man stood before God and asked, "I put all of my faith in You. Why didn't You come and save me?"

And God said, "Son, I sent you a warning. I sent you a car. I sent you a canoe. I sent you a motorboat. I sent you a helicopter. What more were you looking for?"

This is a funny story, but it contains a valid truth. Let's be careful not to miss our rescue. We are promised protection, but we need to move when He tells us to. It is also important to note that we cannot put God to a foolish test. When we deliberately put ourselves in harm's way, when we walk in areas we have no business being in, and when we do stupid things we know are dangerous and disregard the warnings, we can't assume God will come to our rescue.

Jesus knew that you don't test God. And like Him, you need to be wise to the enemy's temptations. Satan had the audacity to try to tempt Jesus by twisting Scripture. How much more will he try to deceive you? You must understand that the enemy also knows the Bible, and he will try to manipulate the very promises of God to make you do things you shouldn't.

> *You must understand that the enemy also knows the Bible, and he will try to manipulate the very promises of God to make you do things you shouldn't.*

> *"If you are the Son of God," he said, "throw yourself down. For it is written: "'He will command his angels concerning you, and they will lift you up in their hands, so that you will not strike your foot against a stone.'" Jesus answered him, "It is also written: 'Do not put the Lord your God to the test.'"*
> – Matthew 4:6-7

Satan was correct. He knew Psalm 91 and its promises too. But do you see how he tried to use it as a way to get Jesus to step outside of the will of God. This is not a new tactic for Satan. He started with Eve in the garden, leading her to sin, and he has been trying to prey on women ever since. How many times in your life have you tested the Lord? How many times have you walked outside God's will, thinking that His protection would be your safety net if you went too far? This is not the intention of the Scripture, nor should it be the intention of our hearts. Our hearts should long to live in obedience to our Heavenly Father, not pushing the envelope to see how far we can go and remain under His protection.

Remember, a woman who dwells in the shelter of the Most High is in sync with God's heart. She is confident of His plans for her life, is able to discern the tactics and strategies of the enemy, and is unwilling to compromise who she is. She is surrounded by His presence as she continually spends time with Him. She knows what His promises are for her, and she receives them by faith. ❧

GOING DEEPER

1. Do you believe that angels are literally on assignment watching over you? Prayerfully reflect on all the times His angels have surrounded you and kept you out of harm's way.

2. The spirit world is more real than what we actually observe with our natural eyes. Does knowing there is a spiritual battle taking place all around you scare you or give you peace?

3. Looking at the angels who were sent to rescue Lot and his family, why is it important not to delay obedience? Are there areas in your life right now where you have delayed moving when God has asked you to move? What is causing the delay?

4. God promises to send His angels out to protect us? Does that mean we can do anything and be safe? What does it mean to put God to the test?

She Loves Me

"Because he loves me," says
the LORD, "I will rescue him;
I will protect him, for he
acknowledges my name."

–Psalm 91:14

She loves me; she loves me not. As a child, I used to recite this silly poem as I plucked the petals off, one by one, from the daisies and black-eyed Susans that grew in my yard. I never really put much thought into this poem until recently. The idea behind it is that the "plucker" seeks to determine whether the one he truly loves reciprocates his affection. It's kind of sweet when you think about it. Being loved is such a special gift. One that God also desires from us.

When we were created, we were all given free will. This means that we have a choice whether or not we will love

God. Love is not really love if it is demanded or forced. Our Heavenly Father so desires genuine love from us that He gave us the ability to reject Him and not love Him at all. Psalm 91:14 points out one of the promises that is in store for a woman who willfully chooses to love God with all her heart, not because she has to love Him, but because she is truly enamored with her Creator.

We often talk about and focus our attention on God's love for us. One of the most widely known Scriptures in the Bible is found in John 3:16, "For God so loved the world that he gave his one and only Son, that whoever believes in him shall not perish but have eternal life." Football players write it on their cheeks. Fans hold signs with it in the stands. Billboards line our highways highlighting this powerful verse. God loves us infinitely. His love isn't something we can earn, or lose for that matter. He loves us unconditionally.

However, we don't give as much attention to the reciprocation of that love and how God feels when we choose to love Him above all other things. So many people have rejected His love and His gift of salvation. His intention was to spend eternity with us so that He can take care of us and spend time with us. That's His desire. And for those who have willfully chosen to love Him, that's our guarantee. With that, there are immeasurable promises in store.

One of these promises is highlighted in Psalm 91:14: "'Because he loves me,' says the Lord, 'I will rescue him.'" It's remarkable to actually think about that. My Heavenly Father will rescue me simply because I love him. As I look back at my life, I can clearly see God's faithful hand doing just that so many times—situations that could have gone terribly wrong, times where I didn't see a way out, or times when I put myself in a dangerous situation. God's hand was in all of it, rescuing me and giving me solid ground to stand on. When I reflect on His angels protecting me, I also wonder how many times He rescued me when I didn't even know I needed rescuing. But one thing I know for sure is that God has been and always will be the hero in my damsel-in-distress story.

> *He lifted me out of the slimy pit, out of the mud*
> *and mire; he set my feet on a rock and*
> *gave me a firm place to stand.*
> – Psalm 40:2

This verse so resonates with me. He rescued me from a life of regret and anguish that day in Las Vegas when He kept my daughter safe as she paraded along the busy passageways of the Venetian hotel. He rescued me from a life of sickness and pain when He spoke to me in the doctor's office that desperate day, reassuring me that He had the last word in my health battle. He rescued my mother and me as we drove through possibly the most unsafe neighborhood in my state, redirecting us to a safe exit. He rescued me as a tornado ripped down my street, keeping my home, family, and me unscathed throughout the storm. The list goes on and on. But most importantly, He rescued me from eternal separation from Him because two thousand years ago, Jesus died on that cross for me.

He Even Rescues the Prostitutes

Imagine being introduced for the first time by your sin, rather than your name. This is exactly how Rahab, the prostitute, enters the pages of Scripture. Although this is how she is first presented, this is not at all how she is remembered. The transformation in her life and her steadfast commitment to a God she barely knew chronicles her in the hall of faith (Hebrews 11).

It was a tumultuous time in Shittim, more specifically Jericho, where Rahab lived. The Israelites, under Joshua's direction, sent two young spies to scope out the city and report back their findings regarding their future opponent. It was inevitable. Jericho was about to get invaded, and not just by anyone, but by the nation of Israel. Stories of God's miraculous exploits were well-known throughout the area, and the people of Jericho were rightfully terrified.

> *"I know that the LORD has given you this land and that a great fear of you has fallen on us, so that all who live in this country are melting in fear because of you. We have heard how the LORD dried up the water of the Red Sea for you when you came out of Egypt, and what you did to Sihon and Og, the two kings of the Amorites east of the Jordan, whom you completely destroyed. When we heard of it, our hearts melted in fear and everyone's courage failed because of you, for the LORD your God is God in heaven above and on the earth below."*
>
> – Joshua 2:9-11

Although Rahab didn't know God personally, she knew of God and His mighty power. So, when the two young spies ended up at her house, she made a deal with them. She would keep the men and their whereabouts hidden under one condition—spare her life and the lives of her family members. The men agreed. All she needed to do was place a scarlet ribbon in the window of her home, have her family remain inside the house, and she and her loved ones would be rescued. Once again, we see in the scarlet ribbon a foreshadowing of the blood Jesus Christ would shed on the cross and the covering it would provide. This was no exception.

As promised, God delivered Jericho into the hands of the Israelites. When the Israelites marched through the land, destruction fell throughout the entire city. But because Rahab recognized that the Lord was the true "'God in heaven above and on the earth below'" (Joshua 2:11), she was rescued out of certain death.

Joshua said to the two men who had spied out the land, "Go into the prostitute's house and bring her out and all who belong to her, in accordance with your oath to her." So the young men who had done the spying went in and brought out Rahab, her father and mother, her brothers and sisters and all who belonged to her. They brought out her entire family and put them in a place outside the camp of Israel.

Then they burned the whole city and everything in it, but they put the silver and gold and the articles of bronze and iron into the treasury of the Lord's house.

> *But Joshua spared Rahab the prostitute, with her*
> *family and all who belonged to her, because she hid*
> *the men Joshua had sent as spies to Jericho—and she*
> *lives among the Israelites to this day.*
>
> –Joshua 6:22-25

Rahab had a choice to make. She could have easily turned on these men and told the officials where they were. But she had heard rumors of this God they served and wanted to know Him. In that moment, even while still living in sin, she turned her heart toward the Lord, acknowledged Him as the one and only true God, and put her full trust in Him. As a result, she and her entire family were saved.

> *By an act of faith, Rahab, the Jericho harlot,*
> *welcomed the spies and escaped the destruction that*
> *came on those who refused to trust God.*
>
> –Hebrews 11:31 (MSG)

Loving God Will Cost You

It's important to note that loving God comes at a price. When we choose to love the Lord above all things, it requires some sacrifice on our part. It can be difficult and lonely. As I mentioned earlier, it means holding the unpopular stance, even when it is countercultural. It can also mean taking a strong position when the authority structures placed above you challenge your entire belief system, even if there are consequences.

Shadrach, Meshach, and Abednego knew this challenge all too well. They were stripped away from their homes, family, culture, and religion and were living as exiles in Babylon. These young Jewish men were in a pagan nation, being forced to serve under an evil ruler. King Nebuchadnezzar set up a gold statue ninety feet high, fashioned in his image, and demanded that everyone bow and worship it at certain times throughout the day. Shadrach, Meshach, and Abednego, unwilling to compromise, refused to bow down and worship anything other than the one true God. But disobeying this proclamation from the king meant their life was in jeopardy because anyone who refused to bow would be thrown into a blazing furnace.

"As soon as you hear the sound of the horn, flute, zither, lyre, harp, pipe and all kinds of music, you must fall down and worship the image of gold that King Nebuchadnezzar has set up. Whoever does not fall down and worship will immediately be thrown into a blazing furnace."
– Daniel 3:5-6

Could Shadrach, Meshach, and Abednego simply have gone through the motions and bowed down when the music started? I mean, surely God would understand that their hearts weren't in it, and they were just trying to protect themselves from certain death, right? No, this wasn't even an option in their minds. These young Jewish boys had resolved in their hearts to love their God with all their heart, with all their soul, and all their mind (Matthew 22:37). I'm sure the first and second commandments that they studied as young boys echoed in their minds. There was no way they would dishonor God by bowing down to anything but Him.

> *"I am the LORD your God, who brought you out of Egypt, out of the land of slavery. You shall have no other gods before me.*
>
> *"You shall not make for yourself an image in the form of anything in heaven above or on the earth beneath or in the waters below. You shall not bow down to them or worship them; for I, the LORD your God, am a jealous God, punishing the children for the sin of the parents to the third and fourth generation of those who hate me, but showing love to a thousand generations of those who love me and keep my commandments."*
>
> – Exodus 20:2-6

Well, as you would imagine, King Nebuchadnezzar was furious when he heard that Shadrach, Meshach, and Abednego wouldn't bow down. What other response would you expect from a king who made a ninety-foot statue of himself? He quickly summoned the young men and gave them one more opportunity to worship the image of gold set before them. They refused again, and their fate was sealed.

Here's what I love about Shadrach, Meshach, and Abednego: They didn't refuse the king's decree because they were certain that God would save them. They refused to bow because they would rather die than dishonor the God they loved. What boldness they had even when staring death straight in the face! That's unwavering love. Live or die, they would not abandon their God.

Live or die, they would not abandon their God.

> *"King Nebuchadnezzar, we do not need to defend ourselves before you in this matter. If we are thrown into the blazing furnace, the God we serve is able to deliver us from it, and he will deliver us from Your Majesty's hand. But even if he does not, we want you to know, Your Majesty, that we will not serve your gods or worship the image of gold you have set up."*
> – Daniel 3:16-18

But *because they loved Him*, God rescued them, just as Psalm 91 says. Not only did God save His boys, but He made a spectacle out of it too. The king had them bound and thrown into a furnace that was seven times hotter than normal. This fire was so hot that some of the guards died instantly as they threw them in. As King Nebuchadnezzar looked on with expectancy to watch those young Jewish boys die, he got to see one of the most impressive rescues in history instead. God did not just pull them out, which would have been remarkable on its own, He sent what looked like "a son of the gods" (Daniel 3:25) to jump in the fire with them, shielding them from that blazing fire. Shadrach, Meshach, and Abednego walked around the fiery furnace, unbound and unharmed. And when they were finally pulled out, "the fire had not harmed their bodies, nor was a hair of their heads singed; their robes were not scorched, and there was no smell of fire on them" (Daniel 3:27).

Ladies, God is more than able to deliver you from your fire today. No circumstance is too difficult for Him. That's not even a question. He is all powerful, all knowing, and everything must obey Him. The real question, however, is do you love Him enough to be put into the fire in the first place?

We need to resolve in our hearts that we will love our Heavenly Father more than anyone or anything that this world can offer. No situation, circumstance, or decision should ever change that. He is looking for women who will love Him with everything, not just when it's convenient or when she needs something.

She Who Dwells loves God with a ferocious love. She knows His name and the authority it carries. She trusts Him explicitly with her hopes, her dreams, and her life. Because she loves Him, He will never abandon her. She is confident of that. I'll reiterate it again. Loving God may cost you, but it is worth everything! ❧

GOING DEEPER

1. How do you feel when people love you, not because they have to but because they choose to? Have you ever thought about how God feels when we choose to love Him?

2. So many times, we feel unworthy of God's love for us. Does it give you reassurance knowing that the Lord saw Rahab while she was still living in sin and offered her an opportunity to have a relationship with Him? Choosing God changed her legacy. How has it changed yours?

3. As you read through this chapter, one question stands out the most. Do you, like Shadrach, Meshach, and Abednego, love God enough to be put into the fire? Has this ever been tested before? If yes, what did you learn about God's character throughout the fire?

She Has Learned the Secret

"He will call on me, and I will answer
him; I will be with him in trouble,
I will deliver him and honor him.
With long life I will satisfy him
and show him my salvation."
–Psalm 91:15-16

Back in 2014, I had the opportunity to attend She Speaks, which is an amazing conference for women held by Proverbs 31 Ministries down in Charlotte. I mention this conference because it truly impacted my life. As you would imagine, there was a special anointing of the Holy Spirit that fell on the event. I remember being full of excitement as I arrived at the crowded conference that first morning. Almost eight hundred women eagerly walked into that banquet room filled with the anticipation of what God was going to do in and through each of us over the course of a couple of days. As I maneuvered my way to the front of the room to get the closest seat possible, I finally settled for a seat further back, secretly wishing I was just a little bit closer to the front. But this seat would have to do.

Sometime in the first session, Lysa TerKeurst mentioned that there was a scroll with a Scripture verse placed at everyone's seat. The staff at Proverbs 31 Ministries had spent hours asking God for specific Scriptures to include in these scrolls to bless the women attending. These mighty women of God prayed that the Holy Spirit would direct the right woman to the right seat so that they would get the right Scripture. You see, as I was making my way through the crowded banquet room that morning, I thought my seat was happenstance, but in fact, it was the result of the fervent prayer of some faithful women.

I eagerly opened the scroll to find this verse typed out before me:

> *Let the redeemed of the LORD tell their story—*
> *those he redeemed from the hand of the foe.*
> – Psalm 107:2

Sitting at that seat and receiving this verse was not at all random. The Lord placed me there. He had seen the battle that I had gone through and the victory that I had received, and knew I had a story of redemption to share. He had revealed to me secrets to the Kingdom of God that I learned during my battle with fear and anxiety. These secrets were not just for my benefit, but for all women. In that moment, as I read this Scripture verse, I realized that it was my job to tell my story of redemption and freedom from the lies the devil was whispering in my ears. The Lord wanted me to share how to live a life full of confidence in our Heavenly Father. That's why I am telling my story. Nearly ten years later, I still have that small piece of paper with the Scripture verse on it tucked into the folds of my Bible. It is my reminder to never stop testifying of His goodness and faithfulness. Ladies, if you can learn the secret like I have, you too can live a life of peace and freedom.

I Called; He Answered

Let's go back to the Venetian for a moment. When my daughter wandered off, I thought my life as I knew it was over. As time passed, the thought of finding her seemed to lessen by the second. Anguish flooded my soul. But I called out to my Savior, barely getting His name out, let alone any request. He knew my voice, and He answered me. I used to consider that day one of the worst days of my life. But I later learned that it was a day of victory, not only because my daughter was indeed safe, but because I discovered without a shadow of a doubt that when I call out to my Heavenly Father, He hears me, and He answers.

Have you ever been in a crowded room full of children? In the midst of all the little voices speaking, squealing, and crying, one child can yell out "Mommy," and that child's mother instantly knows that it is her kid calling her. Why? Because a mother always can recognize the sound of her child's voice. The same is true with our Heavenly Father. When we call out, He knows who we are immediately, and He is quick to answer us.

> *I call on the LORD in my distress,*
> *and he answers me.*
> –Psalm 120:1

There are numerous instances throughout Scripture where people have called out to God, and He answered them. We all know the story of Peter having the faith to walk toward Jesus on the water. But we also all know that, after Peter stepped out of that boat in faith, he began to sink. Peter called out to Jesus, and He immediately lifted Peter up and saved him from sinking. Another example is Hannah. She was stricken with sadness because she was unable to conceive. She called out to God in utter desperation, and He opened her womb and blessed her with a child, who later was a prophetic voice for the nation of Israel. Similarly, King Hezekiah wept bitterly before the Lord, pleading for his life. He called out to the Lord for mercy, and God heard him. He healed Hezekiah's body and added fifteen years to his life. We see time and time again how the children of God called out to their Heavenly Father. Each and every time, He faithfully answers them.

Delivered and Honored

When I read through these final verses in Psalm 91, one phrase stands out to me and, if I'm being completely honest, seems a little out of place. I understand God's heart to answer me, deliver me, and save me, but in addition to all that, why does He feel the need to also honor me? I get it, honor is important. I think we all should do a better job of honoring those in authority, those who have taught us spiritually, and those who have had a great impact in our lives. But when it comes to my relationship with God, I feel that all honor and praise should go back to Him. It just seems in this list of all His promises and great love that He has poured out on me, honor isn't also necessary. But that is the kind of God we serve.

When I read through the Scriptures, it's clear that this is exactly what our God does. Let's look at the account of Esther. We remember the heroic actions she took to save the Jewish people throughout Persia. The festival of Purim each year retells this story and celebrates her faith and boldness. Young girls look up to her for inspiration. In fact, as a little girl, my daughter loved to dress up as Queen Esther in all her royal attire and pretend to save people "for such a time as this" (Esther 4:14). I so admire Esther's courage and fearlessness, but it's not Esther who I want to focus on right now. Instead, I'd like focus on her uncle Mordecai.

Esther was an orphan. History suggests that her father died while her mother was pregnant, and that her mother died during childbirth. Her uncle Mordecai took her in as an infant and brought her up in the knowledge of God. King Xerxes, in an emotional rant, strips his current queen, Queen Vashti, of her title and opens up the position to all of the beautiful young virgins in every province. Esther is one of these women and ultimately wins the heart of the king. She is now positioned perfectly for her purpose.

While Esther is the one that typically gets all the credit for saving the Jews from a terrible fate, Mordecai was also working behind the scenes to help stop the horrific annihilation of God's chosen people. It was Mordecai who raised Esther to be a God-fearing woman. It was Mordecai who instructed Esther to keep her family background and nationality a secret. It was Mordecai who uncovered the plan to assassinate the king. It was Mordecai who informs Esther of Haman's evil plot to destroy all the Jews. It was Mordecai who persuaded Esther to use her royal position to stop the decree from happening so that the Jews would be saved and not perish. And God did not forget this. Not only did God deliver Mordecai from the hands of his adversary, but, like Psalm 91:15 states, He honors Mordecai as well.

Haman literally was seconds away from asking the king if he could have Mordecai impaled because he refused to bow before him, withholding the honor Haman thought he was due. Instead, the king demands that Haman parade Mordecai around the city on the king's royal horse, giving Mordecai the honor that God felt was due. Our Heavenly Father has impeccable timing and a great sense of humor, if I might add. Isn't it so reassuring to know that the good things we do that seem to have gone unnoticed and unrewarded, God remembers at the perfect time?

[Haman's] wife Zeresh and all his friends said to him, "Have a pole set up, reaching to a height of fifty cubits, and ask the king in the morning to have Mordecai impaled on it. Then go with the king to the banquet and enjoy yourself." This suggestion delighted Haman, and he had the pole set up....

When Haman entered, the king asked him, "What should be done for the man the king delights to honor?"

Now Haman thought to himself, "Who is there that the king would rather honor than me?" So he answered the king, "For the man the king delights to honor, have them bring a royal robe the king has worn and a horse the king has ridden, one with a royal crest placed on its head. Then let the robe and horse be entrusted to one of the king's most noble princes. Let them robe the man the king delights to honor, and lead him on the horse through the city streets, proclaiming before him, 'This is what is done for the man the king delights to honor!'"

"Go at once," the king commanded Haman. "Get the robe and the horse and do just as you have suggested for Mordecai the Jew, who sits at the king's gate. Do not neglect anything you have recommended."

So Haman got the robe and the horse. He robed Mordecai, and led him on horseback through the city streets, proclaiming before him, "This is what is done for the man the king delights to honor!"

–Esther 5:14; 6:6-11

Not only does God ensure that Mordecai is honored, but He punishes the man who intended to harm him. Haman received the same death he had planned for Mordecai, being impaled on a pole. King Xerxes then, in another act of honor, presents his signet ring to Mordecai, while Esther gives him Haman's entire estate to oversee. God will deliver you as you walk through some of the darkest valleys in life, and He will honor you too. Often, He will prepare a beautiful banquet for you to enjoy as your enemies watch.

Even though I walk through the darkest valley, I will fear no evil, for you are with me; your rod and your staff, they comfort me. You prepare a table before me in the presence of my enemies. You anoint my head with oil; my cup overflows.

– Psalm 23:4-5

Satisfaction of a Long Life

I spent too many years of my life worrying about what was to come—thoughts focusing on what if something bad happened to me or my family. I was truly missing the peace God so eagerly wanted to gift me. Jesus came to this earth to reconcile us to the Father. Sin separated us from God, but Jesus died so that we may spend eternity with Him in Heaven. Some people think that our reward for serving Him faithfully is only that someday we will dwell in His presence in Heaven. But Jesus says in John 10:10, "I have come that they may have life, and have it to the full."

We don't need to wait until we die to dwell with God. We get to do that right here, right now. Then and only then will we live life to the fullest as the Scripture promises.

So, I ask you, are you truly living your days on this earth to the full or abundantly, as some translations state? Or are you crippled with fear, afraid to embrace all the goodness that the Lord has in store for you during your lifetime? Are you overwhelmed by the trials and demands this world brings because you lack time spent resting in His presence? What good is a long life if you are living it bound by the lies of the enemy? You can't do this life correctly if you refuse to dwell with your Creator. It is just that simple.

> *You can't do this life correctly if you refuse to dwell with your Creator. It is just that simple.*

The Lord wants to bless you with a long life, but also a life that demonstrates His saving power. He wants you to thrive, not just survive. God wants to give you a life full of wisdom and counsel to navigate all the situations you encounter. Fear would have you focus on the what-if scenarios, while faith in our Heavenly Fathers knows that He will be with us *even if*. He wants to move in your life and answer prayers because you've spent time laying them at His feet, putting your faith in Him and nothing else. The Lord has a beautiful future for you. Don't let the enemy rob you of the present.

*"For I know the plans I have for you," declares the
LORD, "plans to prosper you and not to harm you,
plans to give you hope and a future."*
– Jeremiah 29:11

As we come to a close with the final verses of Psalm
91, I hope you have learned the peace that comes to a
woman who dwells regularly in the presence of God. The
powerful declarations found in Psalm 91 should remove
all doubt and fear from your heart as you confidently live
out your days trusting Him. Trusting Him means believing that He's got you no matter what storms come your
way. You will remain dry and unscathed by the elements
because He will never leave you.

Remember, you don't need to see how the future
unfolds as long as you make your residence in the Lord.
The enemy will always try to lie and deceive you. You can
count on that, but don't allow him to make you captive
to fear. You are not alone in this battle. Fight hard, my
friend. I'm standing with you!

She who dwells in the shelter of the Most High has
found her identity in Him, and Him alone. She is confident
in her Creator and explicitly and unwaveringly trusts
her life in His precious hands. She rests in His shadow
and has full confidence in His unfailing love. She Who
Dwells has a direct line to the Father because she has
spent countless hours in His presence, talking with Him.
She doesn't hesitate to call on Him, day or night. And she
certainly doesn't go looking to worldly resources to solve
her problems. Instead, when trials or storms arise, she

drops to her knees and calls out to her Father. He is quick to answer her because she is His. She has learned the secret of dwelling with her Heavenly Father and knows that the safest place to be is in the house of the Lord. ✒

Surely your goodness and love will follow me
all the days of my life, and I will dwell in the
house of the LORD forever.

–Psalm 23:6

GOING DEEPER

1. Do you think it is your obligation to share your stories of God's redemption? What have you personally learned from the testimony of other women? How has this changed your life?

2. Go through the Bible and find other stories of individuals who have called out to the Lord. How did God respond? What does this tell you about calling out to the Lord?

3. Why do you think that God wants to give honor to His children? Have you ever been the recipient of this honor? What does this tell you about God's nature?

4. John 10:10 says, "'I have come that they may have life, and have it to the full.'" Do you think living a life bound in fear, anxiety, worry, and mistrust honors Jesus's mission?

5. What steps are you going to take to trust God at His Word? Write down an action plan to break off the habits of the past to walk into the abundant life that God wants to bless you with. Be specific and intentional.

Notes

She Dwells

1. Merriam-Webster, s.v. "dwell (v.)," accessed on January 16, 2024, https://www.merriam-webster.com/dictionary/dwell.

She Rests

1. Roberts, Nicole F. "Despite $65 Billion A Year Sleep Aid Market, Americans Remain Sleep Deprived," *Forbes*, March 20, 2022, https://www.forbes.com/sites/nicoleroberts/2022/03/20/despite-65-billion-a-year-sleep-aid-market-americans-remain-sleep-deprived/?sh=489418e97521.

2. Tori Masters, "Something I have learned from God through my baby," Instagram, June 20, 2023, https://www.instagram.com/p/Cttnpd2uRT2/?utm_source=ig_web_copy_link&igshid=MzRlODBiNWFlZA==.

3. "Stress statistics 2023: How common is stress and who's most affected?" SingleCare, February 23, 2023, https://www.singlecare.com/blog/news/stress-statistics/.

She Trusts

1. Oxford Languages Online, s.v. "refuge (n.)," accessed on January 16, 2024, via Google search engine, https://www.google.com.

2. "Actions to Take When a Tropical Storm or Hurricane Threatens," National Weather Service, National Oceanic and Atmospheric Administration, accessed on January 16, 2024, https://www.weather.gov/safety/hurricane-action.

3. A. W. Tozer, James L. Snyder, comp., *God's Power for Your Life*, Bloomington, MN: Bethany House Publishers, 2013.

4. Roger J. Green, "1738 John & Charles Wesley Experience Conversions," *Christian History*, Issue 28, originally published in 1990, https://christianhistoryinstitute.org/magazine/article/john-and-charles-converted.

5. Jackie Green and Lauren Green-Mcafee, "Leaving a Legacy of Prayer: The Example of Susanna Wesley," FaithGateway, accessed on January 16, 2024, https://www.faithgateway.com/praying-example-susanna-wesley/#.YUjs9i1h3S8.

She Is Safe

1. Quotations in this paragraph and preceding two paragraphs from: Darrin Karcher, "Poultry Capture and Handling," Purdue Extension, March 2018, https://www.extension.purdue.edu/extmedia/AS/AS-642-W.PDF.

2. "The Frog in Hot Water," Moral Stories, accessed on January 16, 2024, https://www.moralstories.org/frog-hot-water/.

3. A Sermon No. 124, Delivered on Sabbath Morning, March 29, 1857, by the Rev. C.H. Spurgeon at the Music Hall, Royal Surrey Gardens.

4. Merriam-Webster, s.v. "pestilence (n.)," accessed on January 16, 2024, https://www.merriam-webster.com/dictionary/pestilence.

She Is Fearless

1. David Wilkerson, "The Ultimate Test of Faith," World Challenge, March 3, 2021, https://www.worldchallenge.org/ultimate-test-faith.

She Watches from Afar

1. Jfrankcarr, "The exact population is a bit unclear. Estimates for the time period fall between 2 and 4 million," StackExchange, June 6, 2012, https://history.stackexchange.com/questions/2275/what-was-the-estimated-population-living-in-egypt-around-1446-bc.

She Declares

1.   Dictionary, s.v. "lord (n.)," accessed on January 16, 2024, https://www.dictionary.com/browse/lord.

She Is Surrounded

1.   Billy Graham, *Angels: God's Secret Agents*, Nashville, TN: W Publishing Group, 1986.

JESSICA LANDMON is an ordained pastor known for taking deep spiritual matters and presenting them in a simple, practical way. She is the founder of Women Get Real Ministries—a ministry dedicated to helping set all women free from the bondage of fear. Jessica has a heart for discipleship and is on a mission to encourage women to find their calling and boldly walk in it. Although known by her close circle as a planner, all that goes out the door when the Holy Spirit asks Jessica to do something. Her prayer each morning is that the Holy Spirit interrupts her plans and invites her to participate in His. Jessica is happily married to her high school sweetheart, Chad, and is blessed with two incredible children. She and her husband have recently become empty nesters and are traveling their way through this new season of life. ✺